Presidential Confidential

PRESIDENTIAL

Confid

ential

Stories of sex, scandal, murder, and mayhem in the Oval Office by

JOHN BOERTLEIN

Printed in the United States of America
Distributed by Publishers Group West
First edition, first printing

CLERISY PRESS
PO Box 8874
Cincinnati, OH 45208-0874

ISBN 978-1-57860-361-9

Edited by
DONNA POEHNER

Cover and interior designed by
STEPHEN SULLIVAN

Layout by
SANDY KENT

Cover photos appear courtesy of
    Richard Nixon: Photofest
    Tempest Storm: John Boertlein
    George W. Bush: Library of Congress
    John Wilkes Booth: Library of Congress

Photos in Presidential Confidential appear courtesy of:
    Library of Congress: 2, 4, 6, 9, 11, 15, 20, 21, 27, 32, 34, 41, 46, 48, 52, 72, 84, 86, 88, 94, 96, 108, 110, 116, 117, 120, 124, 131, 134, 136, 149, 154, 156, 160, 172, 174, 176, 180, 186, 188, 190, 193, 194, 196, 199, 204, 211, 216, 222, 231, 234, 235, 240, 252 (Albert Fall)
    Wikimedia Commons: 62, 64, 76, 78, 80, 169, 208, 252 (Teapot Dome), 281, 316, 317
    Other photos appear courtesy of Photofest: 260 (Richard Nixon); The President's Daughter, by Nan Britton: 124; Penthouse: 165; PhotoDisc: 311; the author's collection: 141, 142

For the men and women of the United States Armed Services,
especially the brave warriors of the
U.S. Army 7th Cavalry 17th Palehorse Squad,
159th Combat Aviation Brigade, and all those assigned to
Operation Enduring Freedom at Jalalabad, Afghanistan

And also for Stewart, Kyla, and Mary Carol

Table of

CONTENTS

Table of

CONTENTS

Acknowledgments

Many thanks to Jack Heffron, without whom this book would not have been possible. Thanks to Steve Sullivan, who created the original design for the book, and thanks also to Sandy Kent who created the page layout. Donna Poehner, Michael Heffron, and Adam Riser found most of the photos, spending many hours in the search, and I am grateful for their efforts. Richard Hunt, Hillary Bond, and Rachel Freytag make up the marketing and publicity department at Clerisy Press, and I appreciate their support in finding an audience of interested readers.

If you don't have a good sense of humor, you're in a hell of a fix when you are president of the United States.—Harry Truman

PART ONE

Assassins, Anarchists, *and* Assorted A'holes

NOTHING SENDS SHOCK WAVES THROUGH the American heart like the murder of a president. Four sitting U.S. presidents have been killed while serving in office. Six others have survived assassination attempts. In Part I, we'll take a look at the people, motivations, and conspiracy theories associated with these deadly deeds.

If Lincoln were alive today, he'd probably roll over in his grave. —Gerald Ford

Since I came to the White House, I got two hearing aids, a colon operation, skin cancer, a prostate operation, and I was shot. The damn thing is I've never felt better in my life.—Ronald Reagan

Being president is like being a jackass in a hailstorm. There's nothing to do but to stand there and take it.—Lyndon B. Johnson

President Andrew Jackson

1

A Tough Nut to Crack

Andrew Jackson

IT WAS A COLD DAY IN WASHINGTON ON January 30, 1835, as President Andrew Jackson made his way from his White House office to the U.S. Capitol building to pay his respects at the funeral of a congressman who had passed away. The Capitol rotunda held a crowd, gathered in hopes of getting a glimpse of the President. One of the onlookers, however, held malice in his heart.

Richard Lawrence, a young drifter, had two pockets full of pistol. As people made way for President Jackson to pass, Lawrence lunged out of the crowd while pulling one of the pistols. Lawrence pulled the trigger and a loud explosion echoed through the rotunda. For a tense moment, everything fell silent—nothing happened. The bullet never left the gun. A misfire.

Jackson, a crusty old soldier with quick instincts, went after Lawrence with his walking cane. Lawrence managed to back away and produced the second pistol. At close range, aiming for the President's heart, Lawrence squeezed the trigger. Nothing. Another misfire!

Some men from the crowd, including Davy Crockett, the Tennessee congressman, tackled Lawrence and held him on the ground. Jackson continued flailing his cane, trying to crack the would-be assassin's skull. His aides had to pull him away and whisk him back to

"Old Hickory" Jackson proved to be a crusty old cuss. When whack-job-would-be-assassin Richard Lawrence's pistols both misfired, the President opened a can of whoop-ass on the guy with a little assistance from onlookers in the Capitol Rotunda.

Hostage!

AS ANGER BETWEEN NORTHERN AND SOUTHERN states boiled in 1860, Texas senator Louis Wigfall hatched a scheme to kidnap President James Buchanan. A volatile, violent man, Wigfall wanted Buchanan out of the way so Vice President John Breckinridge would take over. Breckinridge, from Kentucky, would be much more sympathetic to the Southern cause—and he did join the Confederacy when war finally broke out a year later. After he was kidnapped, Buchanan's life would be used as leverage in negotiating a deal favorable for the South. Wigfall, however, had burned many political bridges during his career and could not muster enough support for the plan to make it happen. Buchanan remained safe. Plans to kidnap the president became regular news during Lincoln's administration. ✪

the safety of the White House. The President was safe. The attempt had failed. Andrew Jackson dodged the bullet—twice. Firearms experts figure the chances against two misfires in a row are about a lottery-sized 125,000 to 1.

At his trial, Richard Lawrence, an unemployed house painter, was deemed insane. His motive for attacking President Jackson, he said, was that he, as rightful heir to the British throne, wanted to punish the President for killing his father three years before. The story made absolutely no sense. A jury found Lawrence not guilty of attempted murder for being "under the influence of insanity." Richard Lawrence spent the rest of his life in an insane asylum.

ABRAHAM LINCOLN,
SIXTEENTH PRESIDENT OF THE UNITED STATES.
Born Feb. 12th 1809.   Died April 15th 1865.

President Abraham Lincoln

2

Belonging to the Ages

THE POLITICAL CLIMATE OF 1860 WAS electric with rumors of war, dissolution of the union, and the abolishment of slavery. Plots to kill Abraham Lincoln emerged almost from the time he was elected president. Even before his arrival in Washington, a scheme was uncovered to murder the President-elect. Lincoln took a train from his home state of Illinois to the nation's capital for the inauguration. The specially decorated rail cars were scheduled to stop in several cities en route to inaugural celebrations.

The last stop before Washington was Baltimore, Maryland. It was there, a rail detective learned, that a group plotted to cause a diversion from the celebration by staging a large fight. During the melee, another group would rush the train and stab the President-elect. Railroad officials insisted Mr. Lincoln switch trains, thereby avoiding the crowd and making his way safely through Baltimore at night. Lincoln reluctantly agreed.

News reporters caught wind of the detour and published stories to embarrass the President-elect. They accused Lincoln of "sneaking" into Washington at night and made garish mention of elaborate disguises—when, in fact, Lincoln had merely changed hats. The stories met their mark. Mr. Lincoln said he didn't like "stealing into Washington like a thief in the night," and he swore he would never change plans for safety's sake again. This was a vow he kept throughout his presidency, despite the fact that he received over ten thousand death threats, some of which he kept on his desk in an envelope marked "assassinations," over the next four years.

Despite safety issues, Lincoln always moved freely around Washington. There were sporadic instances where shots were fired at the man, but he remained philosophical, even telling a guard, "I have perfect confidence in those around me, in every one of you. I know no one could do it and get away with it. But if is to be done, it is impossible to prevent it."

Perhaps President Lincoln had a premonition in early 1865 when he told friends about one of his dreams. In it, he claimed, he heard people crying. Wandering around the White House, Lincoln dreamed he saw soldiers in the East Room standing guard over a coffin. He asked the soldiers, "Who is dead in the White House?" "The president," they replied, "he was killed by an assassin." A couple of blocks away, a man named John Wilkes Booth plotted to make the President's dream a gruesome reality.

Twenty-six-year-old John Wilkes Booth was born the ninth of ten children to British immigrants Junius Brutus Booth, a noted stage actor, and his mistress. Mary Ann Holmes. John's parents wed when he was thirteen. The Booths maintained a summer home at John's birthplace, Bel Air, Maryland, as well as winter quarters on Exeter Street in Baltimore. By age seventeen, young Booth had begun establishing himself as an actor in his own right. He also kindled a devotion to national politics of the day. When the Civil War erupted, Booth became a vehement and vocal Confederate sympathizer, loudly denouncing the Lincoln administration and voicing his outrage over Southern status in the war. The actor also strongly opposed the abolishment of slavery in the United States and President Lincoln's proposal to grant voting rights to emancipated slaves.

After the defeat of the Confederacy, Booth gathered a group of co-conspirators to kill Lincoln. They also schemed to murder Vice President Andrew Johnson and Secretary of State William Seward. The assassins believed the slaughter might further the Confederate cause, despite the surrender only days earlier. Confederate General Joseph E. Johnston's army was still in the fight, so, in the minds of the conspirators, the attack on Union leadership would prove devastating to the Union. Booth met three loyal henchmen—David Herold, Lewis Paine, and George Atzerodt—on April 13, 1865, with the mass assassination plan. Atzerodt got cold feet, but Booth assured

Mary Todd Lincoln

him the group would all go to the gallows together if the plan failed. Booth told Atzerodt to rent a room at the Vice President's quarters at the Kirkwood House. Atzerodt complied and immediately proceeded to get drunk.

The next day was Good Friday, but victory celebrations of recent Union victories overshadowed the usual solemnity of the day in Washington. Booth stopped by Ford's Theatre, where rehearsals were in session for the evening performance of *Our American Cousin,* and learned that President Lincoln planned to attend the night's performance.

He saw his chance.

He scouted the theatre, checking the balcony stairs and the presidential box, which overlooked the stage. He watched the actors rehearse, noting times when the audience might be loud with laughter. He checked the door to the box and noticed the lock was broken. He may have made a peephole in the door so he could see the President before entering the box.

Satisfied, Booth left Ford's and returned to his hotel room, where he checked the one-shot brass derringer he needed. He packed a pocket compass, a pocket watch, photographs of several lady friends, and a large sheath knife before leaving to meet with his three accomplices.

At their last meeting, Booth described each of the assassin's jobs. He would shoot President Lincoln and perhaps also be able to stab to death General U.S. Grant, who planned to accompany Lincoln to the theatre. Herold and Paine were assigned to kill Secretary of State Seward. Booth kept the two together because he doubted Herold's resolution and worried that Paine was too stupid to find Seward's house on his own.

Atzerodt was told to kill Vice President Johnson on his own. But Booth doubted he had the moxie, so he manufactured a plot to divert suspicion in the conspiracy toward the Vice President. Booth laid a red herring by stopping by Johnson's hotel and leaving a card

SATAN TEMPTING BOOTH TO THE MURDER OF THE PRESIDENT.

(left) John Wilkes Booth was literally demonized by the Northern press while others in the war-torn nation saw him as a gentlemanly national hero. (below) John Surratt, a conspirator in the Lincoln assassination, wearing a Papal Zouave uniform.

First Lady—Confederate Spy?

DURING THE CIVIL WAR, FIRST LADY MARY TODD Lincoln's family became the subject of an official investigation by a joint committee of Congress. Mary came from a prominent Kentucky family who owned slaves. When war broke out, some of the Todd siblings supported the Confederacy and some the Union. Even though divided families were common, the Todd family drew suspicion.

Several of the Todd boys died while serving in the Confederate army. Mary's sister, Emilie Todd Helm, lost her husband, Confederate General Benjamin Hardin Helm, at Chattanooga. Abraham Lincoln had offered Helm a high-ranking officer's post in the Union army, but he turned it down.

Rumors abounded that Mrs. Lincoln kept the channels of communication open with her Confederate family members and may have passed them information. Eventually, a secret congressional committee formed and started to draw up charges against Mrs. Lincoln. While the committee was in session, the President made a surprise visit. He had not been summoned to testify, nor had he been told of the reason for the investigation. The President read this statement:

"I, Abraham Lincoln, President of the United States, appear of my own volition before this Committee of the Senate to say that I, of my own knowledge, know that it is untrue that any of my family holds treasonable communication with the enemy."

Honest Abe then stood and left the room. The committee summarily dropped the investigation. ✪

12

reading "Don't wish to disturb you. Are you at home? - J. Wilkes Booth." Booth figured even if the Vice President survived, the note would cause enough suspicion and confusion to allow the conspirator's escape and buy time for the Confederacy to rebound.

April 14th was a busy day in the President's office. General Grant attended one meeting, where he gave he regrets to the President that he and his wife were unable to attend the theatre that night after all. President Lincoln acknowledged that he wasn't too interested in going either, but he knew Ford's Theatre had advertised his attendance, and he would not like to disappoint people.

That evening, Abraham Lincoln dressed in the same suit he wore at his second inauguration a month prior. He and Mrs. Lincoln boarded a carriage for Ford's Theatre. They stopped on H Street to pick up the first lady's friends, Clara Harris and her fiancé Major Henry Rathbone, who had agreed to replace the Grants in the presidential box.

Our American Cousin was already under way by the time the Lincolns and their guests arrived. Laura Keene, the star of the show, saw them entering the box and brought everything to a halt while the orchestra played "Hail to the Chief." The audience gave the President a rousing ovation. Lincoln responded with a wave to the crowd and took his seat in a rocking chair placed in the box for his comfort. He told his guard, John Parker, to go find himself a better seat on the floor where he could enjoy the play. Parker left the box, unattended from the outside, and took an aisle seat before he grew bored and decided to step next door for a drink.

At around 9:30, John Wilkes Booth rode his horse up the alley to the stage door. He dismounted and found a stagehand to hold his horse. He entered the theatre and made small talk with some fellow actors while waiting for the moment in the play when the audience would be roaring with laughter. He knew the play well and decided to fortify himself with whiskey before he made his move. He stepped next door to the bar to wait for the appropriate scene.

After some drinks, Booth returned to the theater, this time using the front door. The ticket-taker and he kidded whether he needed a ticket—he didn't. Booth climbed the stairs and made his way down the narrow hallway to the presidential box. There was no one outside when he looked through the peephole to see President Lincoln sitting in his rocking chair, a shawl draped over his broad shoulders. Booth opened the door unnoticed and silently stepped inside, pistol in hand. He heard the line he was waiting for—You sockdologizing old man trap!—and heard the audience burst into laughter. Then he pulled the trigger. Nobody noticed President Lincoln slump forward in his chair.

Mary Lincoln, laughing with everyone else, turned to her husband and thought he had dozed off. Then a dark-haired young man shoved his way past her. Young Major Rathbone lunged from his seat and grabbed the man, but Booth slashed him with his knife. Booth jumped out of the box onto the stage, eleven feet below. An experienced actor, he thought he'd have no trouble making it from the presidential box onto the stage, but Rathbone grabbed him hard enough to upset his balance, and the spurs of his boots apparently caught on one of the flags adorning the presidential box.

Booth's leg twisted and broke as he landed on the stage. He limped to the stage door, mounted his horse, and rode away. Chaos reigned inside the theatre as the crowd realized the President had been shot. Panicked audience members poured onto the street screaming the horrific news.

People in Washington had many reactions. Some wept. Some whooped with joy. A soldier reportedly shot and killed a man for rejoicing over the shooting.

Twenty-three-year-old surgeon Charles Leale, who had graduated medical school just two weeks prior, was first to arrive at the scene. Leale's first thought was that the President was dead. He wasn't breathing, and his eyes revealed signs of severe brain trauma. The doctor ran his hands through the President's hair and located

(right) The derringer Booth used to assassinate President Lincoln. The gun remains on display, as does the presidential box (below) at the Ford's Theatre Museum in Washington D.C.

You sockdologizing old man trap!

THE ASSASSINATION OF PRESIDENT LINCOLN,
AT FORD'S THEATRE WASHINGTON D.C. APRIL 14TH 1865.

the bullet wound behind his left ear. Leale managed to restore the President's breathing, but it was too late. Abraham Lincoln never regained consciousness. He was carried to William Peterson's boarding house across the street from Ford's Theatre by Leale and other doctors and some soldiers who happened to be in the audience.

President Lincoln survived through the night. The first lady had to be taken from the room after throwing herself on her husband in hysterics. Twenty-one–year-old Robert Lincoln arrived and stood vigil at the head of the bed. Lincoln's cabinet members and staff gathered at Peterson's.

Booth's fellow conspirators' plans had failed. Atzerodt never made it out of a saloon where he continued a drinking binge. Herold managed to get Paine to Secretary Seward's house and waited outside while Paine pretended to deliver medicine to the secretary of state. When Seward's son refused to let Paine into his father's bedroom, Paine shot him. Paine had to use his knife on another son and Seward's nurse before he could get at the Seward. When a house-servant ran out screaming, Herold rode off in terror. Paine, thinking he had murdered four people, ran into the street looking for Herold. Discovering he was alone and lost, Paine returned to his own boarding house. Although all four of Paine's victims were seriously hurt, none was killed.

Secretary of War Edwin M. Stanton took charge. Learning of the stabbings at the Seward house, Stanton believed the assaults were a last-ditch effort by the Confederacy to destroy the Union. He immediately ordered the arrest of any persons known to have associated with the young actor who had been identified at Ford's Theatre. Almost three hundred people, including Lewis Paine, were brought into custody by Union troops.

Booth had already escaped. He managed to cross the Anacostia River over the Navy Yard Bridge before guards had been alerted of the shooting. Riding into Maryland, Booth headed to a predetermined spot to join the other assassins. Herold had taken the same route out of Washington and caught up with Booth about an hour later. Booth and Herold traded horses because it looked like Herold's mare might provide a smoother ride for Booth's broken leg.

Booth's leg was causing so much pain he was unable to ride much further. He knew he needed a doctor and headed for the farm of Dr. Samuel Mudd. Mudd owned a spread Booth had once considered buying. But he had a problem. Booth knew the terrain, but he wasn't sure how receptive Dr. Mudd would be to the man who had shot Lincoln. Should he pass Mudd by and try to make it to Virginia, where he was sure he would be greeted as a hero? The pain answered his question and Booth rode to Dr. Mudd's farm.

Before knocking at Mudd's door, Booth attempted to disguise himself as an injured old man. Herold and Booth arrived at Mudd's about four in the morning. Dr. Mudd, no stranger to late-night patients, came out to look at the injured leg. Booth kept his face turned away. With Herold's help, the doctor carried Booth to a spare bedroom where he cut off Booth's boot and splinted his leg. Booth's leg throbbed with pain, but he and Herold managed to ride off from the Mudd's farm by late afternoon. There is much disagreement as to whether Dr. Samuel Mudd ever recognized Booth. At the time, Mudd told a relative about the late-night patient and the relative alerted the authorities, who promptly arrested Dr. Mudd on charges of aiding Booth's escape.

Meanwhile, a silent and solemn crowd gathered in front of Peterson's boarding house. Inside, doctors did what they could. At 7:22 on the morning of April 15, 1865, President Abraham Lincoln died. Edwin Stanton remarked, "Now, he belongs to the ages."

The President's body was laid out in the East Room of the White House, exactly as in Lincoln's dream. Twenty-five thousand mourners filed by the casket in one day. Thousands more paid their respects as the body lay in state at the Capitol building. On April 21, a train draped in black left Washington for Mr. Lincoln's final journey back to Illinois. Thousands of people stood along the railroad tracks as the funeral train passed. Thousands more filed past the coffin at stops in ten cities along the way. Abraham Lincoln was buried near his home in Springfield on May 4, 1865.

Booth evaded capture for almost two weeks. Stanton suspected he was still in Maryland and offered a reward of $100,000 to anyone who turned in the assassin. He also dispatched fifteen hundred soldiers into the Maryland countryside to hunt Booth. A young boy told the army about two fellows who had crossed the Potomac River into Virginia around April 23, nine days after the shooting at Ford's Theatre. The boy's description sounded like Booth and Herold.

The people of Virginia did not give Booth a hero's welcome. Quite the contrary, when Booth contacted Confederates he knew they expressed horror at what he had done. With no friendly harbor to be found, Booth and Herold hid in a tobacco barn in Port Royal, Virginia. Booth's diary contains thoughts of his confusion over the reception in Virginia:

> "I hoped for no gain, I knew no private wrong. I struck for my country and that alone." Americans had "groaned beneath [Lincoln's] tyranny and prayed for this end, and yet now behold the cold hands they extend to me."

On April 27, Federal troops tracked Booth and Herold to the Port Royal barn. When the pair refused to surrender, the soldiers set the barn on fire. Herold ran out and surrendered. Booth responded by rushing forward trying to extinguish the flames. Then he collected some guns and made for the barn door.

There are differing versions of what occurred next. Sergeant Boston Corbett, one of Booth's pursuers, said he feared Booth was about to fire upon the troops, so he fired a shot. Others thought Booth shot himself.

Booth dropped. The soldiers rushed him and dragged him out of the fire. His dying words were, "Tell my mother I died for my country." The body of John Wilkes Booth was moved back to Washington, where it was buried under a prison cell as Union officers didn't want anti-Lincoln sentimentalists to find Booth's grave and make a shrine of it. Booth's body was eventually returned to his family, who buried it in an unmarked grave next to his father's in Baltimore. A headstone at the site is still unmarked today, except for Lincoln-head pennies left by visitors.

After a thorough investigation, eight suspects were scheduled for trial. They included:

- David Herold, who served as guide to the Seward home for Lewis Paine and fled Washington with Booth.
- Lewis Paine (aka Lewis Powell), who seriously wounded Secretary of State Seward, his children, and his nurse.
- George Atzerodt, whose job in the conspiracy was to kill Vice President Andrew Johnson. He got drunk instead.
- Samuel Arnold and Michael O'Laughlin, who had been part of an earlier plot to kidnap the President. Both were suspected of being involved in the murder conspiracy.
- Ned Spangler, the Ford's Theater employee who found someone to hold Booth's horse.
- Dr. Samuel Mudd, who wittingly or unwittingly gave medical aid to John Wilkes Booth.
- Mary Surratt, who ran the boarding house where the conspirators congregated.
- John Surratt, Mary's son, who would have been arrested as a conspirator, but he had left town before the murder. On the night of the assassination, he fled to Canada. From there he went to the Vatican, where he became a member of the papal guard.

The eight prisoners were kept isolated, their legs chained and their heads covered with white hoods to keep them from communicating. Secretary Stanton ruled that the President's assassination was

(far left) We all hang together! Accused conspirators in the Lincoln assassination prepare to stretch the gallows ropes under the watchful eyes of heavy security provided by the Union Army. (above) A cartoon issued not long after the assassination of President Lincoln, showing those who conspired to kill him.
(left) Conspirator Lewis Payne in manacles.

an act of war, meaning that there would be no trial by jury. Nine army officers heard the case in a military tribunal.

The trial began on May 9, only five days after Lincoln was buried. No newspaper reporters were permitted into the closed proceedings. The prisoners were not permitted to testify, and they remained chained and hooded as the cases were heard. After weeks of complaints from the newspapers, the trial was opened to the public. Eventually the prisoners' hoods were also removed.

Mary Surratt, the only woman on trial, received most of the attention. Her lawyer, priest, and daughter all claimed she knew nothing about the murder plot. Prosecutors disagreed. They said most of the conspirators met at her boarding house. They also pointed out that Paine had sought refuge there upon leaving the Seward house. Things didn't look promising for Mary.

On July 6, 1865, the tribunal found all eight prisoners guilty as charged. Ned Spangler was sentenced to six years in jail. Dr. Samuel Mudd, Samuel Arnold, and Michael O'Laughlin received life sentences in the penitentiary. David Herold, George Atzerodt, Lewis Paine, and Mary Surratt were sentenced to hang. Their executions were scheduled for the following day.

Because the government had never hanged a woman, many expected Mrs. Surratt to receive a last-minute pardon from the president. But Andrew Johnson wouldn't relent, saying Mary had "kept the nest that hatched the egg." Mary walked to the gallows with the other convicts on July 7, even though Lewis Paine shouted, as they placed the noose around his neck, "Mrs. Surratt is innocent. She doesn't deserve to die with the rest of us." The four swung from one gallows.

The question of whether Abraham Lincoln's survival could have unified a divided country with peace, equity, and prosperity continues through the ages.

3

Are You Employed, Sir?

James Garfield

TO THE VICTOR GO THE SPOILS! IN 1881 THE the "victor" was James A. Garfield, the twentieth president of the United States. As "victor," President Garfield was charged with administration of "the spoils," which included every government appointment and job. Whenever a new president was elected, political patrons packed the White House seeking a piece of the government pie.

President James Garfield

In those days, the general public had access to the offices of the White House. When James A. Garfield moved in, thousands of favor-seekers crowded the corridors, most in hopes of getting a government job. One person in the crowd seeking Garfield's favor was a thin, bearded man named Charles Julius Guiteau.

Thirty-nine-year-old Charles Guiteau was somewhat of a drifter. Originally from Chicago, Guiteau had failed at a number of jobs. He tried being a lawyer, a writer, a lecturer, a theologian, and a bill collector, but nothing worked out. He spent money he didn't have and accumulated incredible amounts of debt. He was quick to anger and an avowed wife-beater. When his wife divorced him, her testimony horrified the judge so much he ordered Guiteau to never marry again.

During the 1880 presidential election, Guiteau's newest interest became international politics. He decided his destiny lie as ambassador for his country to one of the great courts of Europe, the Austro-Hungarian Empire. Guiteau figured if he could pick the winning side of the presidential election, the ambassador's job would be his. A sign of gratitude for his popular support—easy as that.

So Guiteau picked the experienced Republican Ulysses S. Grant, even writing a speech about the former president and Union general. He was disappointed when the Republicans chose Ohio senator James Garfield as their candidate instead.

Guiteau recovered from the disruption by amending the campaign speech slightly. He simply changed "President Grant" to "Senator Garfield" at every mention of the candidate. The fact that the two men had a lot in common (both were from Ohio and both served as Civil War generals) made it easy on campaigner Guiteau. After delivering the speech at a Republican rally in New York, Guiteau relaxed and waited for the election.

When Garfield won, Guiteau figured he was as good as on his way to Austria. He packed his bags and headed to Washington to claim his prize, arriving two days after President Garfield's inauguration. Guiteau made his way to the White House, where he was surprised to find the hallway and grounds already crowded with fellow office-seekers waiting in line to claim their government jobs.

Guiteau hated waiting his turn. Besides, he'd given a speech, right? He cut line and shoved his way into a room where Garfield was meeting with other men. Guiteau was unceremoniously led out of the room before he could get a word in with the President. He was insulted but not discouraged.

Guiteau began hanging around the White House, making frequent attempts to contact the President by leaving notes or messages with aides, in which he offered advice and services. He was undaunted when he learned another man was appointed ambassador to the Austro-Hungarian Empire and graciously agreed to accept another position: a counsel general in Paris.

Guiteau waited weeks, and weeks turned to months—still no word from the President's office. He'd been such a nuisance that White House staff had been told he "should be quietly kept away." A secretary suggested he try his luck at the State Department. After managing to get a couple of meetings with Secretary of State James Blaine, Guiteau was kicked out of the State Department as well.

During the endless round of rejections, Guiteau kept up with newspaper reports about New York Senator Roscoe Conkling's ongoing dispute with President Garfield about passing out government jobs to the various states. Conkling led a group of Republicans known as the Stalwarts. His idea was for the President to grant the Senator the authority to assign patronage jobs to the Stalwarts in New York State. But Garfield insisted on making the appointments himself.

At first Guiteau wrote letters to the President supporting his stance. But then the politico wanna-be began to think about the dozens of frustrated fellow office-seekers he'd met in Washington. He postulated that the legion of unhappy job seekers might start another civil war! This time the war would start over the methods

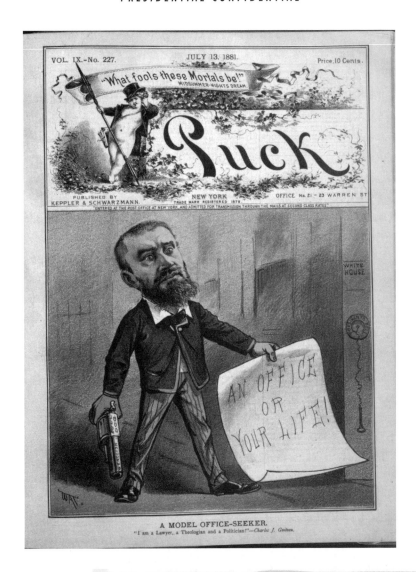

This cartoon accurately portrays Charles Guiteau's twisted reason for murdering James Garfield. When Charlie didn't get his place on the public nipple, he decided to speed the attrition process by using a gun.

used to grant government jobs. The country needed to be saved, once again, from itself!

"I was thinking over the political situation," Guiteau later wrote, "and the idea flashed through my brain that, if the president was out of the way, everything would get better."

In the beginning, the idea of killing President Garfield horrified Guiteau. But reflection on the matter convinced him that God had planted the idea in his head, and so it was God's will that Garfield die. The delusion that he would become a national hero, to be rewarded with a coveted government job by Vice President Chester Arthur, made the idea of murder even more appealing.

In early June, Guiteau purchased a pistol and a box of ammunition. Realizing he might face jail time before he could be rescued by the new president, Chester Arthur, Guiteau scouted the facilities at the District of Columbia jail. He liked the lock-up, calling it "the best jail in America."

Believing most Americans would want to know more about the man who rescued their country from another civil war, Guiteau began revising *The Truth, a Companion to the Bible*, a book he had written several years earlier.

With his purpose clear, Guiteau began stalking President Garfield. He armed himself and followed Garfield to church, to the train station, and even to the secretary of state's house. He couldn't seem to find his opportunity. He was tempted to pull the trigger once, but Garfield's ailing wife, Lucretia, was nearby and Guiteau lost his nerve.

When Mrs. Garfield left town for the seasonal beaches of New Jersey, Guiteau followed the President more closely and read of Garfield's plan to join his wife and younger children on the Jersey shore for a Fourth of July celebration. From there, the Garfields would travel to New England to attend the President's reunion at William's College in Massachusetts. They might even return for a visit to Ohio.

Guiteau realized he needed to act on his plot or risk waiting for months. The newspapers reported the President's departure was scheduled for 9:30 on the morning on Saturday, July 2. Guiteau would be there.

On the night before, Guiteau sat in his boardinghouse writing a letter of explanation for what he was about to do. He woke early on July 1 and strolled down by the Potomac River for some target practice with his revolver. Then he made his way to the Baltimore and Potomac Railroad Depot at Sixth and B Streets, where he waited for President Garfield's arrival.

The President also woke up early the morning of July 2. The first four months of his presidency had taken their toll, and he was ready to escape for a vacation. One problem he'd been unable to solve was the enormous number of people seeking government jobs. He tried to be fair, but there just weren't enough jobs to fill the demand. The newspapers estimated that there were twenty applicants for every position. Garfield could not escape the angry majority he couldn't accommodate. He wrote in his journal, "Some Civil Service Reform will come by necessity after the wearisome years of wasted Presidents have paved the way for it."

Secretary of State Blaine picked up the president at 9:00 A.M. in his carriage for the short ride from the White House to the train station. Arriving early, the two chatted in the carriage before entering the station off the B Street side at about 9:20. They walked through the ladies' waiting room toward the main passenger area when two gunshots rang out behind them. One bullet grazed President Garfield's coat sleeve. The other hit him in the back. The President's hands reached for the air, he screamed, "My God, what is that?" and slumped to the floor. Blaine turned and saw Guiteau with the smoking gun and immediately charged the gunman, who was tackled by a police officer.

"I did it and will go to jail for it," Guiteau said. "Arthur is president now, and I am a Stalwart." Other officers arrived and hustled him off to the police station. The cops failed to search Guiteau until they arrived at the station. There they found the gun still in his pocket. They also found two letters Guiteau had written. One contained instructions for the army to seize the jail he would soon call home. The other was addressed to the White House and read: "The President's tragic death was a sad necessity, but it will unite the Republican Party and save the Republic."

Meanwhile, President Garfield lay bleeding on the train station floor. The bullet had entered near his spinal column. Dr. Smith Townsend, a District health officer, happened to be at the station and attended to the President. Even though Townsend was certain the wound was fatal, he told the President it didn't look too serious so as not to frighten him. "I thank you, doctor," Garfield replied, "but I am a dead man."

A mattress was brought in from a sleeping car to carry the President to a second-floor office. More doctors arrived, but there was nothing they could do. Garfield requested to return to the White House. He was loaded into a horse-drawn ambulance and taken home, followed by a procession of horrified onlookers.

President Garfield suffered through three operations, one without benefit of anesthetics. Doctors were unable to locate the bullet (the autopsy revealed it had entered the pancreas). Antibiotics had not yet been discovered, and the president battled infections and high fevers. For a while, despite the physicians' doubts, Garfield seemed to improve, to the point of making the journey from Washington to Long Branch, New Jersey, (his original destination), where he could escape the summer heat and convalesce in the ocean breeze. He even managed to sit up for the first time since the shooting. But the fever persisted.

Eighty days after the shooting, on the evening of September 19, 1881, President James A. Garfield succumbed to the assassin's bullet. The nation had followed the gruesome ordeal closely from the beginning, and everyone seemed to share Garfield's mother's sentiments when she said, "If he had to die, why didn't God take him without all the terrible suffering he endured?"

The President's body was removed to Washington, where it lay in state at the Capitol Building rotunda for two days. From there, a funeral train was commissioned to remove the President back to Ohio. Thousands of people lined the tracks along the way, dropping flowers as the train passed.

The nation had watched Garfield suffer throughout the summer. Now their attentions switched to Charles Guiteau, who sat in solitary confinement inside the D.C. jail. He had not yet been charged with a crime as authorities waited to see if President Garfield would survive. By now, Guiteau realized Chester Arthur was not going to help him. Instead of being hailed a hero, he realized his only fame came in the many rumors of lynch mobs. Even the jailers despised him. One of his guards shot at him but missed. Others reportedly plotted to torture him before they hanged him. Guiteau began to worry about his trial and his future.

He knew his trial would be expensive so, in true Guiteau fashion, he wrote a letter to the White House soliciting cash. Guiteau reasoned that President Chester Arthur owed him money. After all, he said, his actions had made it possible for Arthur to get a significant increase in salary from a Vice Presidential $8,000 a year to a Chief Executive's $50,000. There was no response from the new president or from the White House.

Having briefly practiced law himself, Guiteau decided to defend himself. He concocted three defenses for his actions: First, James Garfield died in the state of New Jersey, hundreds of miles from the jurisdiction where the alleged crime occurred. Second, Garfield had lived for eighty days after the alleged assault—the shooting only contributed to the man's demise. (Guiteau claimed the actual cause of death was incompetent medical care.) Finally, Charles Guiteau wasn't responsible for the shooting because he was only acting under the orders of God.

Guiteau realized he needed help at the defense table, but no one wanted the job. He finally had to settle for George Scoville, his brother-in-law and a lawyer with no experience in criminal law. Two other attorneys eventually joined Scoville, but he remained lead counsel and did most of the talking.

Scoville wisely abandoned the New Jersey argument immediately. He was willing to place some of the blame on medical malpractice, but he realized his only chance was to plead not guilty by reason of insanity. Most people had to agree Guiteau must be insane. Even President Garfield expressed that opinion before he died. At his trial, Guiteau did nothing to prove otherwise. He muttered to himself and mocked the judge. He flagrantly argued with witnesses and court officials, sometimes even his own lawyers. He loudly protested he was not insane but that God had destroyed his free will.

On January 25, 1882, after seventy-one days at trial, the jury left to deliberate. Less than an hour later, the verdict returned: Guiteau was guilty of murdering the President of the United States.

Four months later, on June 30, 1882, nearly a year after he pulled the trigger, Charles Julius Guiteau swung from the noose-end of the hangman's rope.

Guiteau stalked President Garfield until he saw his opportunity at a Washington train station. After Guiteau bushwhacked Garfield, an angry crowd subdued the cowardly attacker. The police finally took Guiteau into custody and proceeded to botch the investigation.

4

Another Century's Terrorists

William McKinley

IN THE LATE NINETEENTH CENTURY, EUROPE'S monarchies were plagued by radicals with murder on their minds. In a twenty-year span, political anarchists (those who see no need for government and seek to overthrow those that exist) carried out assassinations on a number of the crowned rulers of various countries. Alexander II of Russia died in a suicide bombing. The president of France and the empress of Austria were stabbed to death. A gunman shot and killed the king of Italy. All in the name of anarchy.

President William McKinley

But America is an ocean away from Europe. Why would anarchy be a problem in the cradle of democracy? No one here was born into a rigid class system, and our leaders were elected by the populace. Americans didn't see a problem with fanatic anarchists here—until the summer of 1900. It was then that an investigator looking into assassination of Italy's King Umberto I came across a list of six names of political leaders who anarchists planned to murder. The first three people on the note were already dead, the fourth had survived several attempts on his life, and the fifth name sent a chill through Washington—William McKinley, president of the United States.

The President's staff had lived through the assassinations of Abraham Lincoln and James Garfield, and they took the threat seriously. Despite the earlier assassinations, security around the president still was lax. The Chief Executive usually rode or walked around the city without guards. The anarchist's note, however, prompted the staff to ask for protection from an unlikely source.

The Secret Service started as a spy agency during the Civil War to detect counterfeit money and stamps. Its mission seemed a long way from guarding the President. But the void was obvious, and Secret Service agent George Foster was assigned to protect the Chief Executive. President McKinley despised the idea of a constant guardian and frequently gave Foster the slip for a private walk or carriage ride with the first lady. When he visited his home in Canton, Ohio, McKinley insisted on privacy—unguarded privacy. But Agent Foster took the job very seriously. He was often seen jogging alongside the presidential carriage, alert for any signs of trouble.

Meanwhile, in the Ohio farmland, twenty-eight-year-old Leon Czolgosz was becoming obsessed with the violent political climate in Europe. The son of a Polish immigrant, Czolgosz repeatedly read the stories of assassinations on his father's native continent. He admired the anarchist's motives, believing monarchy was the enemy of the working masses. And the enemy, he thought, deserved to die. He grew angry at the stories of anarchists who failed in their missions, certain they had missed their targets by shooting from too far away so they could more easily escape. A real anarchist, Czolgosz believed, was not concerned for his own safety. He should shoot from close range, and be ready to surrender and accept his fate as a martyr to the cause of anarchy.

By the spring of 1901, Czolgosz decided to put his new beliefs into practice. He cashed in his share of the farm and began to travel in the name of anarchy. In May he went to Cleveland to hear a lecture by noted anarchist Emma Goldman. Czolgosz was impressed. "Miss Goldman's words went right through me," he later said, "and when I left the lecture, I had made up my mind that I would have to do something heroic for the cause I loved."

Czolgosz even traveled to Chicago to meet Goldman, who found little time for the young man. His attempts to join organized anarchist groups or movements also failed. He found the groups either uninterested in his help or, in some cases, suspicious that he was a government spy. The radical pro-anarchy newspaper *Free Society* even printed a warning to the faithful:

> The attention of the comrades is called to another spy. He is well dressed, of medium height, rather narrow shouldered, blond, and about 25 years of age. Up to the present he has made his appearance in Chicago and Cleveland. In the former place he remained a short time, while in Cleveland he disappeared when the comrades had confirmed themselves of his identity and was on the point interested in the cause, asking for names, or soliciting aid for acts of contemplated violence. If this individual makes his appearance elsewhere, the comrades are warned in advance and can act accordingly.

But Czolgosz remained adamant. He read in a Chicago newspaper about President McKinley's plans to attend the Pan-American

Exposition in Buffalo, New York. The exposition's theme was "a century of progress," and McKinley was scheduled for a speech on international trade. Czolgosz dropped the paper and headed for the train station—bound for Buffalo.

Upon arrival, Czolgosz discovered crowds eagerly anticipating McKinley's visit. The exposition had declared September 5, the day of McKinley's speech, as "President's Day." Disgusted by the scene, Czolgosz later said: "All those people seemed to be bowing to the great ruler. I made up my mind to kill that ruler. I bought a .32-claiber revolver and loaded it."

The President arrived at the fairgrounds September 3, and Czolgosz was waiting. But the crowd was enormous, and people pushed forward to get a glimpse of "President Mac." Police officers corralled the mob, keeping them back. Czolgosz couldn't get close enough to shoot the President and later complained, "They forced everybody back, so the great ruler could pass." He stalked the President for the next two days. It's been suggested that Czolgosz hesitated to act because he feared retaliation from the crowd or the police. He disputed the claim, saying, "I was not afraid of them, or that I would get hurt, but afraid I might be seized and my chance would be gone forever."

On day four of the exposition, Czolgosz found out the President would be attending a public reception at the large and ornate Temple of Music. He arrived early to get a place in the front of the reception line.

The President's advisors hated the idea of a "public reception." In fact, McKinley's personal secretary, George Cortelyou, had taken it off the schedule twice. But McKinley, politician that he was, insisted on attending. Cortelyou asked Secret Service agent Foster to bring in extra soldiers to guard the aisles of the Temple of Music. Ironically, the soldiers also blocked Foster's view of the people standing in line to meet the President.

The east entrance of the Temple of Music opened at 4:00 on the afternoon of September 6, 1901. People entered two by two and lined up single file as the aisle narrowed. President McKinley stood on a raised platform, shaking hands. On that hot day, some used handkerchiefs to mop the sweat from their brows, and so it didn't seem unusual when Leon Czolgosz pulled a handkerchief from his pocket. Cortelyou, standing near the president, noticed the cloth—and the bulge under it—but assumed the man's hand was injured and bandaged. He was more worried about a suspicious-looking fellow in line ahead of Czolgosz.

Agent Foster also noticed the other man and eyed him closely. He moved near the man and walked beside him as he approached the President. Cortelyou and Foster both took a breath of relief when the man shook the President's hand and walked on. Next, the President greeted a little girl and her mother. He shook the woman's hand and gave the girl's head a friendly pat. Then he turned with a smile and extended his hand to Leon Czolgosz.

Czolgosz shoved the President's hand aside and fired two shots through the handkerchief covering his gun. The Temple of Music fell silent. McKinley stood still, staring blankly at his assailant. Foster and two other men, including the man who had drawn such suspicion, tackled Czolgosz and wrestled him to the floor. William McKinley took a step backward, then turned and walked to a chair a few feet away. Cortelyou rushed to the President's side as more people piled on Czolgosz, some threatening to hang him there and then.

The President responded by muttering, "Don't let them hurt him."

"But you are wounded!" Cortelyou answered, "Here, let me examine."

"No, I think not," McKinley said. "I am not badly hurt, I assure you." Cortelyou noticed a blood stain spreading across the President's white linen shirt. "My wife," whispered the President. "Be careful, Cortelyou, how you tell her...oh, be careful."

An ambulance arrived within minutes, and the medical team rushed McKinley to a temporary emergency hospital constructed for the exposition on the fairgrounds. The "hospital" was actually little more than a first-aid station, but the doctors decided the President needed immediate surgery. One bullet dropped out as attendants removed his clothing, but the other had penetrated his abdomen. President McKinley recited the Lord's Prayer as they administered ether. When the surgeons cut in, they found the second bullet had torn through the stomach. They repaired the holes but couldn't find the bullet. Ironically, the exposition featured a display of a new medical device called an X-ray machine, but the attending physicians apparently didn't know its capabilities so it wasn't tried.

As dusk set in, they rigged an electric light to finish the surgery. The doctors seemed optimistic as the President was removed to the home of John Milburn, president of the exposition, whose house was located on the fairgrounds.

Hundreds of people kept vigil outside the Milburn house. Reporters set up tents across the street with telegraph machines to send news about the President across the country. Vice President Theodore Roosevelt and the President's cabinet members rushed to Buffalo. By the time they arrived, doctors reported President McKinley was "on the high road to recovery." They predicted he would be back to work in three to four weeks. "Good news! Good news!" one doctor told reporters five days after the shooting. He said the President's wounds had healed and there were no signs of blood poisoning. The President seemed to be doing better. He was sitting up and talking. He told his wife and Cortelyou, "It's mighty lonesome in here," during a visit to his room.

Then, on September 13, the doctors reported a "sinking spell." Antibiotics were still not available, and gangrene set in along the bullet's path. Since the shooting, McKinley was receiving nourishment by liquids through a tube in his rectum, but his body began rejecting everything. His condition worsened as he drifted in and out of consciousness. Near the end, the President came to for a moment and gathered the attending doctors around his bed. "It is useless, gentlemen," he told them. "I think we ought to have a prayer." He asked for his wife and took her in his arms. "It is God's way," he told her. "His will, not ours, be done." Then he began to whisper the words of a favorite hymn, "Nearer, My God, to Thee."

William McKinley, twenty-fifth president of the United States, died at 2:15 on the morning of September 14, 1901.

The autopsy revealed that President McKinley died of gangrene. The second bullet was never recovered. Doctors said it was probably lodged in the fatty tissue of the back. A funeral train was commissioned to bring the President's body back to Washington. Thousands of people waited in the streets, some singing "Nearer, My God, to Thee."

Like Abraham Lincoln and James Garfield before him, William McKinley's body lay in state in the White House East Room and the Capitol Building rotunda. On the day of the funeral, thousands of people rushed to get inside the rotunda, and three hundred mourners were crushed. Nobody died, but the Capitol Building offices had to be converted to a hospital of sorts, with almost every room used for emergency care. After the funeral, President McKinley's body rode the funeral train to its final resting place in Canton, Ohio.

Czolgosz remained unremorseful throughout the ordeal. "I am an anarchist," he affirmed. "I am a disciple of Emma Goldman. Her words set me on fire." His words set a grieving nation on fire. They didn't do any good for Emma Goldman either. A nationwide search began for the infamous, now-despised anarchist. Four days after the shooting, Goldman was arrested in Chicago using an assumed name. "I never advocated violence," she said, "I scarcely knew him [Leon Czolgosz]." At first held without bail, Goldman was later released when no evidence of a conspiracy could be found.

Czolgosz was held at New York's Auburn Prison. Within an hour of the President's death, Auburn's warden began receiving requests to witness Czolgosz's execution. The trial wasn't even scheduled yet.

No lawyer wanted anything to do with defending Czolgosz. Finally, two reluctant retired judges were drafted into service. Czolgosz's trial began on September 24, just ten days after the President's death, in Buffalo, New York. It lasted eight hours and twenty-six minutes. It only took thirty-five minutes more for the jury to reach a verdict: guilty. First Degree Murder. A little over a month later, on October 29, 1901, Leon Czolgosz was strapped into New York's electric chair and fried. Authorities poured carbolic acid into Czolgosz's coffin so his body would disintegrate within twelve hours.

(below left) It happened at the World's Fair. . . . Well, not exactly. William McKinley bought it in a public reception line at the Pan-American Exposition in Buffalo, New York. (below right) Commie assassin Leon Czolgosz does the perp walk prior to getting the hot seat in New York's electric chair. Carbolic acid was poured into Czolgosz's coffin after to dissolve the body within twelve hours.

The Presidential Twenty-Year Curse

BEFORE BECOMING A U.S. REPRESENTATIVE AND Senator from Ohio, and eventually the ninth president of the United States, William Henry Harrison found fame as an Indian fighter. Defeating a loosely knit group of tribes led by the Shawnee Chief Tecumseh at the Battle of Tippecanoe earned Harrison the nickname "Old Tippecanoe."

Two Native American leaders of the Shawnee tribe, Tecumseh and Tenskwatawa ("The Prophet"), resisted the encroachment on their land by organizing a confederation of like-minded Native Americans of various tribes to fight westward expansion. In 1811 Harrison, then territorial governor, assumed command of an army to march against any Indian uprising. He earned his nickname after victory at the fierce battle at Prophetstown, next to the Wabash and Tippecanoe rivers.

The defeat foiled Tecumseh's plan to organize resistance, and the chief grew bitter toward Harrison. For his part, Old Tippecanoe saw his victory as a political feather in his cap that could help him achieve higher office. Tecumseh sided with the British in the War of 1812 and died at the Battle of the Thames at the hands of American soldiers who were once again commanded by Harrison. According to Joel Martin and William J. Birnes, authors of *The Haunting of the Presidents*, Tenskwatawa, Tecumseh's younger brother, despised Harrison and all he stood for.

Tenskwatawa was known among the Shawnee as a prophet and a holy man with remarkable paranormal abilities. He deeply resented the white man's westward movement and instructed his followers to avoid settlers, who he described as "children of the Evil Spirit." To William Henry Harrison, the Prophet was an "imposter." According to Martin and Birnes, Harrison said, "If he really is a prophet, ask him to cause the sun to stand still, the moon to alter its course, the rivers to cease to flow, or the dead to rise from their graves. If he does these things, you may believe he has been sent from God."

Tenskwatawa answered the challenge when, remarkably, he predicted a solar eclipse that partially covered the sun. He also forewarned of an earthquake that struck the Midwest on December 16, 1811. The event was of such magnitude "the Mississippi and Ohio Rivers flowed backwards." Followers and enemies alike began to take Tenskwatawa's magic more seriously.

Many did not scoff then when the Prophet placed a curse upon the American presidency. He went on to describe how Harrison, if he were to become the "Great Chief," would die in office. "And when he dies you will remember my brother Tecumseh's death," *The Haunting of the Presidents* quotes Tenskwatawa as saying, "And after him, every Great Chief chosen every twenty years thereafter will die. And when each one dies, let everyone remember the death of our people."

"Tippecanoe and Tyler Too!" was the campaign slogan that lead William Henry Harrison to the White House in 1840. He departed his home in Cincinnati in late January of 1841 and was inaugurated on March 4. Some say he caught his death of cold that day but, whatever the case, four weeks later he became the first sitting U.S. president to die in office when he succumbed to pneumonia at the age of sixty-eight, a mere month after the inauguration. Tenskwatawa's prophesy was realized.

But what of the Shawnee medicine man's "Twenty-year curse?" History provides the startling answer:

- Abraham Lincoln—Elected in 1860, assassinated in 1865.
- James Garfield—Elected in 1880, assassinated in 1881.
- William McKinley—Elected in 1900, assassinated in 1901.

- Warren G. Harding—Elected in 1920, died of a sudden illness three years into his first term in 1923.
- Franklin Delano Roosevelt—Elected to a third term in 1940, died in office in 1945.
- John F. Kennedy—Elected in 1960, assassinated in 1963.
- Ronald Reagan—Elected in 1980, survived an assassination attempt in 1981. One might conclude he broke the curse, though some say his fatal Alzheimer's disease may have begun during his final term as president. Others believe he may have survived John Hinckley, Jr.'s assassination attempt because first lady Nancy Reagan consulted astrological charts prior to the scheduling of all of her husband's appointments and helped him to literally dodge a bullet. Mrs. Reagan has never publicly confirmed or denied this practice.

President George W. Bush, elected in 2000, also survived, so perhaps the curse has been broken at last—though only the ghost of Tenskwatawa knows for sure. ✪

5

Hunting the Bull Moose

Theodore Roosevelt

THEODORE ROOSEVELT SERVED THE remainder of William McKinley's term as president, after which he was elected to another four-year term. He left the White House in 1909, and his friend and Secretary of War, William Howard Taft, took office. When the primaries of 1912 came around, "Teddy" found he had issues with several of Taft's political views. He decided to throw his hat in the ring once again. The Republican Party, however, saw little benefit in abandoning the incumbent and re-nominated President Taft. The Democrats backed former college professor Woodrow Wilson. T.R. responded by forming his own political entity—the Bull Moose Party.

President Teddy Roosevelt

Roosevelt was traveling to Milwaukee for a campaign rally on October 14, 1912, when a man leapt out of a crowd, produced a pistol, and shot the former president in the chest. The bullet blasted through Roosevelt's coat, his steel spectacle case, a folded fifty-eight-page copy of the speech he was to deliver, and lodged in his ribcage. People in the crowd seized the shooter, threatening to lynch him on the spot until Roosevelt yelled, "Stand back! Don't hurt that man!"

Despite a bloodied shirt and a bullet in his ribs, Roosevelt decided to deliver the speech. Later, he went to a hospital and had the annoyance extracted. Taft and Wilson announced they were suspending their campaigns until Teddy recuperated.

While everyone admired Teddy's courage and resilience, division in the Republican Party and the Bull Moose took their toll on both parties, and Woodrow Wilson was elected president.

The gunman, identified as former New York City saloonkeeper John F. Schrank, told authorities the ghost of William McKinley ordered him to shoot Theodore Roosevelt. Shrank was deemed insane. Even though millions of Americans wanted him executed, Schrank was committed to the Central State Mental Hospital in Waupun, Wisconsin, for thirty-one years. Schrank's health eventually failed, and he died on September 16, 1943.

6

A Little Luck for the President-Elect

IN THE EARLY 1930S, AS THEY ARE TODAY, presidential elections were held on the first Tuesday in November, but inaugurations took place in March of the following year. FDR had time on his hands during the winter of '33, so he decided to take a fishing vacation with friends in Florida.

On February 15, 1933, the President-elect gave an impromptu speech from the back of an open car in the Bayfront Park section of Miami, Florida, the home of a young Italian immigrant, Giuseppe Zangara. Zangara, like many others in the Depression era, was unemployed and living off of what savings he had managed to accumulate. He decided to make a drastic statement.

Zangara joined the crowd at the park, armed with a .32-caliber pistol he bought at a local pawnshop. However, being only five feet tall, he was unable to see Roosevelt over the crowd of people, so he stood on a wobbly folding metal chair, peering over the hat of Lillian Cross, the hundred-pound wife of a Miami doctor, to get a clear aim at his target. He pulled the trigger five times. After the first shot, Cross and others grabbed his arm, and he fired four more shots wildly. He missed the President-elect, but five other people were hit, including Chicago mayor Anton Cermak, who was standing on the running board of the car next to Roosevelt. En route to the hospital, Cermak allegedly told FDR, "I'm glad it was me and not you, Mr. President," words now inscribed on a plaque in Bayfront Park.

President Franklin Delano Roosevelt

In the Dade County Courthouse jail, Zangara confessed and stated in broken English, "I have the gun in my hand. I kill kings and presidents first and next all capitalists." He pled guilty to four counts of attempted murder and was sentenced to eighty years in prison. As he was led out of the courtroom, Zangara scolded the judge, "Four times twenty is eighty. Oh, judge, don't be stingy. Give me a hundred years." The judge, aware that Mayor Cermak might not survive his wounds, replied, "Maybe there will be more later."

Cermak died of peritonitis nineteen days later, on March 6, 1933, two days after Roosevelt's inauguration. Zangara was promptly indicted for first-degree murder. He pled guilty to the additional murder charge and was sentenced to death. After hearing his sentence, the killer stated, "You give me electric chair. I no afraid of that chair! You one of capitalists. You is crook man too. Put me in electric chair. I no care!"

On March 20, 1933, after only ten days, Giuseppe Zangara was executed in "Old Sparky," Florida State Penitentiary's electric chair. Before he fried, Zangara became incensed when he learned no newsreel cameras would be filming his execution. His last words were:

> "Get to hell out of here, you son of a bitch. I go sit down all by myself. Viva Italia! Goodbye to all poor peoples everywhere! Lousy capitalists! No picture! Capitalists! No one here to take my picture. All capitalists lousy bunch of crooks. Go ahead. Push the button!"

7

Sleeping in His Underwear

IT WAS 1948 AND THE WHITE HOUSE, like America, had suffered through the Great Depression and the long years of World War II. Government engineers inspected the Executive Mansion and declared it in danger of collapse at any moment. The current occupants, the Truman family, were forced to move across the street to Blair House during renovations. The repairs took more than three years to complete.

President Harry Truman

The Secret Service found Blair House a challenge to protecting President Truman and his family. It was much smaller than the White House and much closer to the street. On typical hot and humid Washington days, only a screen door separated President Truman from people on the sidewalk. November 1, 1950, was one of those hot days.

Since air conditioning was not yet available, the temperature inside the house was just as high as outside. President Truman stripped to his skivvies and stretched out on his bed in an upstairs bedroom to relax with the windows open, but his rest was violently interrupted by the sound of gunfire in the street. Two men, Griselio Torresola and Oscar Collazo, attacked Blair House from different sides, guns blazing, intending on murdering the President.

"A president has to expect these things"

Torresola and Collazo were members of the Puerto Rican Nationalist Party. The Nationalist Party rejected political participation through balloting and advocated violent resistance to the U.S. government. The Nationalists were angered by what they viewed as great injustices against Puerto Rico, a United States territory. They viewed Puerto Rico as a colony demanding independence.

Torresola had walked up Pennsylvania Avenue from the west side while his partner, Collazo, engaged Secret Service agents and White House policemen with his Walther P 38 pistol from the east. When Torresola approached a guard booth at the west corner of Blair House, he saw Officer Leslie Coffelt sitting inside. Torresola assumed a shooting stance, and pivoted from around the front of the booth, firing four shots from his 9 mm German Luger. Three of the shots struck Coffelt in the chest and abdomen, the fourth went through his uniform. Coffelt slumped wounded in his chair.

A Peculiar Institution

HARRY TRUMAN WAS ONE OF OUR MOST QUOTABLE presidents. More than most, he was able to step back and see the position clearly and to provide insight into it. Herewith, ten observations from "Go Get 'Em Harry":

1. The presidency is the most peculiar office in the history of the world.
2. Being president is like riding a tiger. A man has to keep on riding or be swallowed.
3. To be president of the United States is to be lonely, very lonely, at times of great decisions.
4. The United States has never suffered seriously from any acts of the president that were intended for the welfare of the country. It's suffered from the inaction of a great many presidents when actions should have been taken at the right time.
5. First, he should be an honorable man. Then he should be a man who can get elected. Finally, he should be a man who knows what to do after he is elected.
6. You have got to know something to be president. You have got to be a jack of all trades and know something about all of them.
7. The president spends most of his time kissing people first on one cheek and then on the other in order to get them to do what they ought to do without getting kissed.
8. A man in his right mind would never want to be president if he knew what it entails. Aside from the impossible administrative burden, he has to take all sorts of abuse from liars and demagogues.
9. A president may dismiss the abuse of scoundrels, but to be denounced by honest men, honestly outraged, is a test of greatness that none but the strongest men survive.
10. The president of the United States hears a hundred voices telling him that he is the greatest man in the world. He must listen carefully indeed to hear the one voice that tells him he is not. ✪

Torresola then turned his attention to plainclothes White House policeman Joseph Downs. Downs, who had just spoken with Coffelt, proceeded down a walkway to a basement door at the west end of the Blair House when he heard shots being fired. Downs noticed Torresola, but the gunman shot him in the hip before he could draw his weapon. Downs turned back toward the house. Torresola fired two more times, striking Downs once in the back and once in the neck. Downs staggered to the basement door and managed to make it inside, denying Torresola entry. He then headed for the shoot-out between Collazo and several other officers. Torresola saw wounded policeman Donald Birdzell beading down on Collazo from the south side of Pennsylvania Avenue. He managed to shoot Birdzell in the left knee from a distance of approximately forty feet.

Out of ammunition, Torresola stood on the left of the Blair House steps and reloaded. In the meantime, President Truman went to his second floor bedroom window and looked outside. He saw Coffelt stagger out of his guard booth, lean against it, and aim his weapon at Torresola, standing about twenty feet away. Coffelt squeezed the trigger and fired, hitting Torresola in the head and blowing a portion of his brains out. Torresola died instantly. Coffelt later succumbed to his wounds.

"A president has to expect these things," President Truman told the nation. He showed equal calm when he commuted Collazo's death sentence to life in prison.

8

Doomsday in Dallas

WILLIAM HENRY HARRISON STARTED A GRIM
trend in the president's office when he died of pneumonia in 1840 only four weeks after his inauguration.
Every twenty years thereafter, until John F. Kennedy
was elected in 1960, U.S. presidents expired in office: Abraham Lincoln (elected in 1860), James Garfield (elected in 1880), William McKinley (re-elected
in 1900), Warren G. Harding (elected in 1920), and
Franklin D. Roosevelt (re-elected in 1940). After the
1960 election an astute reporter reminded President-
elect Kennedy of the eerie Twenty-Year Curse, but JFK
took it in stride. "That's one tradition we'll have to
break," he quipped.

By 1960 the Secret Service was expert in protecting dignitaries, including the president and his family, but it was a violent age and no one could guarantee that the Chief Executive would remain free from harm. He—and the United States as a whole—had many enemies.

The Cold War raged throughout the world. Early in his presidency, Kennedy dispatched "military advisors" to third-world countries, including Vietnam, in an effort to stymie the spread of communism.

When communist leader Fidel Castro seized power on the island of Cuba, ninety miles south of Key West, Florida, Kennedy took the action as a threat to American security and approved a military invasion, known as the "Bay of Pigs," to restore democracy to the island nation. It failed. Tensions grew between the President and the Soviet Union. When intelligence sources revealed Soviet nuclear weapons in Cuba, Kennedy demanded their immediate removal. The Soviet refusal to comply led the President to appear on national television to firmly warn the American public of the imminent possibility of nuclear war. The Soviets acquiesced and removed the missiles. Jack Kennedy won a showdown with communism. But, as Kennedy fought the politics of communism, a man in New Orleans embraced it.

Lee Harvey Oswald was born in October 18, 1939, in New Orleans, Louisiana. His father, Robert Edward Lee Oswald, Sr., died two months before Lee was born. His mother, Marguerite Frances Claverie, raised Lee and his two older brothers on her own. Before the age of eighteen, Oswald lived in twenty-two different homes and attended twelve different schools around New Orleans; Covington, Louisiana; Dallas, Texas; and in New York City. He lived in a foster home for a year in 1942–1943 when his mother was too poor to take care of him and his brothers. As a child, Oswald became withdrawn and temperamental. Early trouble with the law prompted a court-ordered psychiatric evaluation that described Lee as having a "vivid fantasy life, turning around the topics of omnipotence and power, through which he tries to compensate for his present shortcomings and frustrations." Doctors diagnosed the fourteen-year-old as having a "personality pattern disturbance with schizoid features and passive-aggressive tendencies." They recommended continued psychiatric intervention.

In January 1954, his mother decided to return with Oswald to New Orleans. The psychiatric treatments stopped.

Oswald left school after the ninth grade and never received a high school diploma. Dyslexic, young Lee had difficulty spelling and writing coherently, yet he read voraciously. Through the books he read, he discovered Marxism around the age of fifteen. He wrote in his diary, "I was looking for a key to my environment, and then I discovered socialist literature. I had to dig for my books in the back dusty shelves of libraries." The next year, Oswald wrote the Socialist Party of America, stating his dedication to Marxism, which he had studied for "well over fifteen months." He requested information about the Marxist Youth League, though it's unknown if he ever applied.

Lee Oswald enlisted in the U.S. Marine Corps on October 24, 1956, one week after his seventeenth birthday. As a Marine, Oswald trained in the use of the M1 Garand rifle. His proficiency rating as of December 1956 was 212, two points above the minimum for qualifications as a sharpshooter. In May 1959, on another range, Oswald scored 191, one point above the minimum ranking for marksman. He trained as a radar operator, even managing to be granted security clearance from the military.

Oswald didn't hesitate to tell fellow Marines about his anti-American beliefs, but despite his political views, one of Oswald's officers, Lieutenant John Donovan, rated Oswald as "very competent." The young Marine subscribed to *The Worker*, the Communist Party newspaper, and claimed to have taught himself basic Russian. However, a later Marine proficiency exam in written and spoken Russian was rated "poor."

In the fall of 1959, Lee got a hardship discharge from the Marine Corps by exaggerating his mother's "poor" health. After visiting his mother for a couple of days, he executed a plan to immigrate to Russia. By October, the nineteen-year-old was off to Eastern Europe. He managed to get a passport by submitting several fictional applications to foreign universities, through which he obtained a student visa. The Soviet consulate in Finland issued a visa on October 14. He left Helsinki by train on the following day, crossed the Finnish-Soviet border at Vainikkala, and arrived in Moscow on October 16, 1959.

He applied for Soviet citizenship right away, but on October 21 his application was refused. Oswald proceeded back to his hotel bathtub where he slashed his left wrist with a razor, causing a bloody but minor cut. After he received medical care for the superficial injury, he was kept by the cautious Soviets for psychiatric observation at a hospital.

Oswald next went to the United States Embassy in Moscow, where he renounced his U.S. citizenship. From there he returned to Soviet officials claiming, he had been a radar operator in the Marine Corps and that he would make known to them such information concerning the Marine Corps and his specialty as he possessed. He intimated that he might know something of special interest.

When the Navy Department heard of Oswald's scheme, it promptly changed his Marine Corps discharge status from "hardship/honorable" to "undesirable."

Although Oswald had wanted to remain in Moscow and attend Moscow University, he was sent to Minsk, now the capital of Belarus, where he received a job as a metal lathe operator at an electronics factory. He lived in a rent-subsidized, furnished apartment where, in addition to his factory pay, he received monetary subsidies from the Russian Red Cross Society.

His life fit Soviet-era working-class standards, but he remained under constant surveillance by the KGB during a thirty-month stay in Minsk.

After settling into the local lifestyle, Oswald met and soon after married Marina Prusakova, but he gradually grew bored with life in Russia. He wrote in his diary in January 1961: "I am starting to reconsider my desire about staying. The work is drab, the money I get has nowhere to be spent. No nightclubs or bowling alleys, no places of recreation except the trade union dances. I have had enough." Shortly afterward, Oswald sought to negotiate with the U.S. Embassy in Moscow about returning to the United States. After nearly a year of paperwork and waiting, on June 1, 1962, Lee left Russia, taking Marina Oswald, and their daughter, June, to Texas.

Life in the United States wasn't easy for the Oswalds. Lee couldn't maintain a job and he began abusing his wife. He wanted to be noticed. He wanted to be important. He decided to speak out in a dramatic way—with violence.

As a Marine, Oswald trained in

General Edwin Walker was an outspoken anti-communist, segregationist, and member of the John Birch Society. He had been commanding officer of the Army's 24th Infantry Division based in West Germany under NATO supreme command until he was relieved of his command in 1961 by JFK for distributing right-wing literature to his troops. Walker resigned from the service and returned to his native Texas. He became involved in the movement to resist the use of federal troops for securing racial integration at the University of Mississippi, resistance that led to a riot on October 1, 1962 in which two people were killed. He was arrested for insurrection, seditious conspiracy, and other charges, but a local federal grand jury refused to indict him.

Oswald considered Walker a "fascist" and the leader of a "fascist organization." In March 1963, Oswald purchased by mail order a 6.5 mm caliber Carcano rifle and a revolver, using the alias "A.

Hidell." He decided to kill the fascist. Oswald went to Walker's house and located the retired general sitting in his dining room. Oswald set up less than one hundred feet outside and fired at him through the dining room window. Walker survived only because the bullet struck the wooden window frame, which deflected its path. He was shot in the forearm by bullet fragments. The police had no leads, and the incident received little notice in the press. Oswald was armed and still at large.

Lee Oswald remained a zealous communist despite feeling betrayed by the cool reception he had received in the Soviet Union. He changed his attention to the relatively new communist country of Cuba, believing Fidel Castro was more pure of politics. The Bay of Pigs attack, perpetrated by President Kennedy, outraged Lee Oswald. He founded the "Fair Play for Cuba Committee" and took to

the use of the M1 Garand rifle.

street corners with pamphlets demanding "Hands Off Cuba!" He took his message to his hometown of New Orleans, where he went searching for a job. Failing that, he decided to travel to Cuba.

The United States government forbade travel to Cuba as part of a federal embargo. Oswald went to Mexico City, believing the Cuban or Soviet Embassies there would aid him in reaching his destination. Neither government was interested in granting the young American entry into Cuba. Disappointed but not dissuaded, Oswald went home to his family in Irving, Texas, to think of other ways he could bring notoriety to himself and his beloved communist philosophy.

Lee confided in Marina that he planned to shoot former Vice President Richard Nixon, who had a reputation as a fierce anti-communist. Then he told her he would hijack an airliner to Cuba. Leaping around their apartment in his underwear, Lee demonstrated

Wanting to greet his adoring public, JFK unwittingly made himself an easy target by riding in an open convertible on a parade route through downtown Dallas.

how he would take the airplane. "Junie," Marina Oswald told the couple's daughter, "our papa is out of his mind."

During this time, Marina discovered she was pregnant with their second child. Lee still had no means of supporting his family until he traveled to Dallas and found work at the Texas School Book Depository. During the week, Lee lived in a boarding house, returning to Irving on weekends to see his family.

Oswald had worked in the book depository for a month when

he read a newspaper article about President Kennedy visiting Dallas on November 22. The paper also published the route the presidential motorcade would take through the city. Oswald couldn't help but notice that the motorcade would pass right by his workplace, and his warped mind went to work. Jack Kennedy, the man who had shown so much contempt for Cuba, was a much more enticing target than a retired army general or a former vice president. Oswald's vision of his place in history began to clarify in his mind.

Oswald returned to Irving on Thursday, November 21. Marina was surprised to see him in the middle of the week. She was even more surprised the next morning when he was gone. All she found was his wedding ring and $170, their life savings, on the bedroom dresser. She didn't know Lee's rifle went with him.

Oswald apparently concealed his firearm in paper he'd stolen from the book depository. When a co-worker picked him up for work the morning of the November 22, Lee told him the package was filled with curtain rods.

JFK's security team knew about dissension in Dallas. There were posters and newspaper ads actually accusing Kennedy of treason. One ad even portrayed Kennedy with a bull's-eye on his forehead. There were bad vibes in Dallas. But the President insisted on going, in large part to solidify support for the upcoming 1964 election. The Democrats in Texas were battling, particularly Governor John Connelly and Senator Ralph Yarborough.

JFK also needed to get himself and wife Jackie out of Washington. Three months earlier, their baby boy, Patrick, had died when he was only two days old. They were devastated. Mrs. Kennedy uncharacteristically went into seclusion and avoided the public spotlight. A trip to Texas would be the family's first time on the road together since Patrick's death.

On Thursday, November 21, 1963, the President and first lady departed Washington and flew to San Antonio, Texas. From there they made visits to Houston and Ft. Worth. They met cheering crowds everywhere they went. There was an occasional negative poster or shouted insult, but by and large Texans loved the young President and his sophisticated wife.

After a night in Ft. Worth, on November 22, the Kennedys made the ten-minute flight to Love Field in Dallas. A bouquet of yellow roses awaited Jackie at the airport. Texas Governor John Connally and his wife, Nelly, picked up the Kennedys in the presidential limousine to begin the motorcade through downtown Dallas. The limo was equipped with a protective bubble-type top, but the President had it removed so he would have better exposure to the crowd. The motorcade included fifteen extra cars and three buses carrying Secret Service agents, presidential aides, news reporters, photographers, and high-ranking Texas Democrats. The procession followed the route Lee Harvey Oswald had read about in the paper.

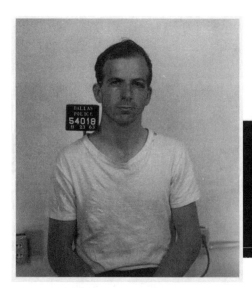

(left) Lee Harvey Oswald's mug shot taken in Dallas after shooting JFK. (below) An M-1 Garand rifle like the one Oswald used to snipe President Kennedy.

The motorcade was scheduled to pass the Texas School Book Depository at 12:25 in the afternoon. Most of the employees joined the cheering crowds lining the street, but one onlooker, standing across the street from the building, noticed a man still standing inside the building on the sixth floor at a window. He was holding a rifle. The gawker assumed the rifleman was a Secret Service agent. He pointed out the man in the window to his wife.

Just before 12:30, Kennedy's limousine entered Dealey Plaza and slowly approached the Texas School Book Depository. Mrs. Connally turned around to the President, who was sitting behind her, and commented, "Mr. President, you sure can't say Dallas doesn't love you." "No," he replied, "you can't."

As the limousine passed the Depository continuing down Elm Street, shots rang out. The majority of witnesses recall hearing three. Initially, the crowd hardly reacted, many later saying they thought the noise was a firecracker or the exhaust backfire of a car. President Kennedy and Governor Connally, sitting beside his wife in front of the limousine, both turned abruptly from left to right. Connally immediately recognized the sound of a high-powered rifle. "Oh, no, no, no, no" he said as he turned farther right, and then started to turn left, looking for the President behind him.

As President Kennedy waved to the crowds on his right, his right arm upraised on the side of the limo, a bullet struck his upper back, penetrated his neck, and exited his throat. He raised his clenched fists to his neck leaning forward and to the left. The same bullet hit John Connally in his back, chest, right wrist, and left thigh. "My God, they are going to kill us all!" he shrieked.

As the limousine passed in front of the John Neely Bryan north pergola concrete structure, a final shot rang out. A fist-size hole exploded out the right side of President Kennedy's head, covering the interior of the car and a nearby motorcycle officer with blood and brain tissue. Jackie Kennedy screamed, "My God! I've got his brains in my hand."

The limo driver sped off. Mrs. Kennedy crawled onto the trunk. Some think she was trying to retrieve part of the President's exploded skull. Others believed she was trying to escape. Still others think she was trying to help a Secret Service agent who was trying to board the speeding car. (Jacqueline Kennedy later said she couldn't remember anything about the action.)

Upon arrival at Parkland Memorial Hospital, the President still had a faint pulse. Doctors performed a tracheotomy and heart massage. They considered opening his chest to perform the massage directly but noticed about one-third of the President's brain was blown away. At one o'clock, John Fitzgerald Kennedy was pronounced dead.

After he shot President Kennedy, Oswald hid the rifle behind some boxes and fled the scene through the Depository's rear stair-

"My God! I've got his

well. About ninety seconds after shooting the President, he ran into Dallas police officer Marion Baker and Roy Truly, his supervisor, in the second-floor lunch room. Truly identified Oswald as an employee, and Baker let him pass. Oswald descended the front staircase and left through the front entrance onto Elm Street just before the police sealed off the building. He was the only employee who left the building after the assassination. His supervisor later noticed him missing and reported his name and address to the police.

At about 12:40, Oswald boarded a city bus. Due to heavy traffic, he requested a bus transfer and got off the bus. He took a taxi to his boarding house. At about 1:00, he went to his room, put on a jacket, grabbed his pistol, and left. His housekeeper, Earlene Roberts, testified that "he was walking pretty fast—he was all but running."

About half a mile away, Dallas Patrolman J. D. Tippit encountered Oswald on a residential street in the neighborhood of Oak

Cliff. He pulled up next to Oswald and spoke to him through a passenger side window. When Tippit exited his squad car, Oswald pulled a .38 caliber revolver and shot the officer four times, killing him in front of two eyewitnesses. Seven other witnesses heard the shots and saw the gunman flee with the revolver still in his hand.

A few minutes later, Oswald ducked into the entrance alcove of a shoe store to avoid passing police cars, and then he slipped into the nearby Texas Theater without paying for a ticket. Johnny Calvin Brewer, the shoe store's manager, had been listening to the day's events on the radio and felt that Oswald was acting suspiciously. Brewer followed Oswald into the theater, where he alerted the ticket clerk, who phoned the police.

The police quickly arrived and entered the theater. After turning on the houselights, Officer Maurice N. McDonald approached

brains *in my hand.* "

Oswald sitting near the rear and ordered him to stand up. Oswald muttered, "Well, it's all over now" and appeared to raise his hands in surrender, but instead he sucker-punched the policeman. A scuffle ensued, during which McDonald says Oswald pulled the trigger on his revolver, but the hammer came down on the web of skin between the officer's thumb and forefinger, preventing the revolver from firing. Oswald was eventually subdued. As he was led past an angry group of people gathered outside the theater, Oswald shouted he was a victim of police brutality.

At about 2:00, Oswald arrived at the Dallas Police Department building. He was held on suspicion of the shooting of Officer Tippit and was questioned by Detective Jim Leavelle. Afterward, he was booked on suspicion of murdering both President Kennedy and Officer Tippit. By the end of the night, he was arraigned on both charges before Justice of the Peace David L. Johnston.

In the hallway of the police station, Oswald had an impromptu brush with reporters and photographers. "I didn't shoot anyone," he protested, "They're taking me in because of the fact I lived in the Soviet Union. I'm just a patsy!" Later, just after midnight at another encounter with the press, a reporter asked, "Did you kill the President?" and Oswald, who had only been advised of the charge of murdering Tippit, answered, "No, I have not been charged with that. In fact, nobody has said that to me yet. The first thing I heard about it was when the newspaper reporters in the hall asked me that question." As Oswald was led from the room, another reporter asked, "How did you hurt your eye?" The black-eyed suspect answered, "A policeman hit me."

"I hope I killed the son of a bitch. It will save you guys a lot of trouble."

Confident they had their murderer, the police invited members of the media to watch Oswald's transfer from the Dallas Police Headquarters jail to a more secure facility at the Dallas County jail the morning of Sunday, November 24, 1963. Reporters, photographers, and television cameras watched as Oswald, handcuffed to a Dallas detective, was led off the jail elevator and into the mob of newsmen. Suddenly, a local strip club owner named Jack Ruby sprung out of the crowd wielding a .38 revolver. Yelling, "You killed my president, you rat!" Ruby fired the pistol into Oswald's stomach.

Oswald crumpled to the garage floor gurgling in pain. Authorities rushed him to the emergency room at Parkland Memorial Hospital—where President Kennedy and Governor Connally were treated two days before. Oswald was on the operating table within

Lincoln–Kennedy Crazy Coincidences

YOU'VE LIKELY SEEN MANY OF THESE BEFORE, BUT NO BOOK about presidential weirdness would be complete without mentioning the strange coincidences between the sixteenth and the thirty-fourth presidents:

- "Lincoln" and "Kennedy" both contain seven letters.
- Both men were over six feet tall, and both were athletic youths.
- Both were shot in the head on a Friday.
- Both were sitting next to their wives when shot.
- Both were also sitting with another couple, the man of which was wounded during the president's assassination.
- Lincoln was shot at Ford's Theatre, and Kennedy was shot in a Lincoln limousine made by the Ford Motor Company.
- Lincoln was in box seven at Ford's theatre, and Kennedy was in car seven in the Dallas motorcade.
- Both assassins had three names consisting of fifteen letters: John Wilkes Booth and Lee Harvey Oswald.
- Both assassins were killed before going to trial.
- Booth shot Lincoln in a theatre and was captured in a warehouse—well, a barn that doubled as a farmer's warehouse. Oswald shot Kennedy from a warehouse and was captured in a theatre.
- Kennedy's secretary, Evelyn Lincoln (whose husband's nickname was Abe), told the president not to go to Dallas. Lincoln's secretary, John Kennedy, told him to stay home from the theatre.
- Both Lincoln and Kennedy were elected to the U.S. House of Representatives for the first time in '46. They were runners-up for their party's vice-presidential nomination in '56, and were elected president in '60.
- Both men lost a child while serving as president.
- Lincoln had sons named Robert and Edward. Kennedy had brothers named Robert and Edward.
- Both presidents were succeeded by southern Democrats named Johnson who were born in '08. ✪

minutes of arrival at the ER. But the bullet had ripped through major blood vessels in his stomach, and there was no way for doctors to save him. He expired at 1:07 P.M. Meanwhile, in an interrogation room at Dallas Police Headquarters, Jack Ruby said, "I hope I killed the son of a bitch. It will save you guys a lot of trouble."

Since those surreal days in Dallas, many people have questioned whether Oswald acted alone, or if he was part of a conspiracy to kill Kennedy. Theories have fingered numerous perpetrators, while many cling to the belief that the assassination was the work of a single, deranged killer. The murder of John Kennedy has become one of the most studied events in American history.

9

Squeaky and Sara Jane, a Couple of Misfires

GERALD FORD BECAME VICE PRESIDENT IN 1973 when he was selected by President Richard Nixon to replace Spiro Agnew, who was all but kicked out of office for various scandals. Then, in 1974, Nixon resigned under his own dark cloud of scandal and Ford inherited the presidency without ever suffering through a national election. In the interest of politics and the Republican Party, however, Ford threw his hat into the ring for the next election in 1976.

(above) President Gerald Ford (right) Lynette "Squeaky" Fromme, one of Charlie Manson's loyal followers, tried to take a shot at President Ford in 1975. Fortunately for Ford, Squeaky didn't know how to use a semi-automatic pistol, and it didn't fire. Fromme was released from the Federal corrections system in 2009.

TIME

THE GIRL WHO ALMOST KILLED FORD

Ford's campaign for the White House was already in gear on September 5, 1975, when he traveled to Sacramento to give a speech on the important topic of violent crime. The President was pressing flesh outside the statehouse when he suddenly noticed a pistol, pointed at him, just a couple of feet away. Secret Service agent Larry Buendorf also noticed the Colt .45 semi-automatic and immediately knocked it away and tackled the young lady brandishing it. As other agents piled on the would-be assailant, she whined, "It didn't go off, fellas!"

The Secret Service rushed President Ford into the statehouse where he delivered his speech, never once mentioning he was a recent victim of the topic he was discussing.

Meanwhile, the would-be assassin was identified as Lynette Alice "Squeaky" Fromme, a noted disciple of convicted murderer Charles Manson. Squeaky's pistol hadn't fired. There were four live rounds in the magazine, but either she didn't know how to, or didn't know she was supposed to, chamber a bullet before the weapon would shoot. No one ever accused Manson Family members of brilliance, and Squeaky didn't help matters when she offered her explanation for the attempt on the President's life: "Well, you know, when people around you treat you like a child and pay no attention to things you say, you have to do something...I stood up and waved a gun (at Ford) for a reason. I was so relieved not to have to shoot it, but, in truth, I came to get life. Not just my life but clean air, healthy water, and respect for creatures and creation."

For her clumsy attempt on President Ford's life, Squeaky earned a life sentence, though she received parole after serving thirty-four years. She was set free on August 14, 2009, and she walks among us today.

But back to 1975: Gerald Ford's run for the presidency was moving along. The worried Secret Service begged the incumbent to cut back on his travels, but Ford knew public exposure was crucial to winning an election. He often spent sixteen or eighteen hours a day shaking hands and meeting the public. "I have no intention of allowing the government of the people to be held hostage at the point of a gun," Ford said. He did, however, agree to wear a bulletproof vest.

He found the protective vest to be itchy, however, and he didn't always wear it. He wasn't wearing it, for instance, seventeen days after his encounter with Squeaky. On September 22, 1975, as he walked out of San Francisco's St. Francis Hotel, a woman across the street pulled a .38 revolver from her purse and shot at him. Fortunately for the President, the bullet whizzed over his head and ricocheted off a car. Unfortunately for a cab driver sitting in a nearby car, the ricochet hit him in the groin. A former Marine named Oliver Sipple, standing next to the shooter, shoved her hand so she couldn't get another shot off. Secret Service agents swarmed the woman.

Other agents pushed the President onto the floor of his limo and sped off. Seventeen minutes later, Air Force One took off with President Ford safely on board. The assailant was identified as forty-six-year-old Sara Jane Moore, a one-time police informant with a sketchy past. Moore said she didn't know why she shot at the President. Like Fromme, she earned a life sentence.

On December 31, 2007, at the age of 77, Sara Jane Moore was released from prison on parole after serving thirty-two years of her life sentence. Gerald Ford had died from natural causes on December 26, 2006, one year and five days before her release.

10

"Honey, I Forgot to Duck..."

Ronald Reagan

FROM *KNUTE ROCKNE, ALL AMERICAN* TO Bedtime for Bonzo, Ronald Reagan starred in over fifty Hollywood movies. But on March 30, 1981, a movie Reagan had never seen, Taxi Driver, turned out to have one of the largest influences on his life. The Martin Scorsese film tells the story of Travis Bickle, a hero/villain who, besides driving a taxi for a living, stalks political candidates, shoots up bad guys, and rescues a pre-teen prostitute, Iris, who is portrayed by actor Jodie Foster.

When the movie premiered in 1976, John Hinckley, Jr. became one of its biggest fans. Hinckley spent hours in darkened Los Angeles theatres watching *Taxi Driver* over and over. He began to see himself as Travis Bickle. And he obsessed over the Iris character. Hinckley transferred his obsession into feelings of "love" for the real-life Foster, who was now a freshman at Yale University. Hinckley took a trip to the Yale campus and tried to phone Ms. Foster. When he couldn't reach her, he left notes for her. Despite his efforts, they never met.

Jodie Foster was a popular celebrity who received fan mail all the time. But there was something weird about Hinckley's letters that scared her. She left them unanswered and passed them along to her college dean. Hinckley didn't let up. He only grew more desperate for Jodie's attention. He decided to take Travis Bickle's lead and stalk a politician.

Ronald Reagan when he was a movie and television star.

Hinckley started being Bickle with then-President Jimmy Carter. He tracked Carter to Dayton, Ohio, and followed him to Nashville, Tennessee, where Hinckley's guns set off a metal detector at the Nashville airport, leading to his prompt arrest. Hinckley had come within shooting range of President Carter on several occasions, but he always lost his nerve. The election of 1980 switched Hinckley's attention to President-elect Ronald Reagan.

On two occasions, Hinckley took his pistol to Washington, where he mingled with crowds who had gathered to see Ronald Reagan. But when the new President showed up, Hinckley couldn't summon the nerve to pull the trigger. Meanwhile, his crazy obsession with Jodie Foster intensified. He sent more letters, but she still wouldn't reply. Once, he did manage to reach her by phone (and recorded the call), and she told him, "I can't carry on these conversations with people I don't know."

Ms. Foster's response to Hinckley's advances was appropriate, but he felt rejected. Deciding that actions spoke louder than words, he left his parent's home in Colorado and flew to Los Angeles on March 24, 1981. The next day he caught an eastbound bus for Yale University. He wanted to impress the young star and figured shooting her ought to do it. Or, perhaps he'd shoot himself in front of her. He soon discovered he was on the wrong bus. Rather than heading for Yale in New Haven, Connecticut, he was on his way to Washington, D.C.

The bus arrived in Washington on Sunday, March 29, at 5:30 in the morning. He considered catching the next bus to New Haven, but he was tired of traveling. He checked into a Washington hotel to think about his next move. The next day he picked up a copy of the *Washington Star* and noticed a story featuring President Reagan's schedule. The President would be delivering a speech to a conference of the AFL-CIO at 1:40 that afternoon at the Washington Hilton. Hinckley decided to check it out.

He returned to his room, showered and dressed, and then he loaded his gun. His pistol was a .22-caliber, RG-14 six-shot revolver

(right) Actor Jodie Foster unknowingly spawned an obsessed, and ultimately violent, fan—John Hinckley—when, as a young teen, she portrayed a child prostitute in Taxi Driver. (below) The Gipper and Nancy greet the masses from the moonroof of their limo in less guarded days.

that cost forty-seven dollars. Alcohol, Tobacco and Firearms agents later determined that the gun was purchased at Rocky's Pawn Shop in Dallas, Texas. Hinckley loaded it with six "Devastator" bullets, which have lead azide-filled centers inside lacquer-sealed aluminum tips designed to explode on impact. One more detail, and he'd be ready to go—he sat down and wrote another letter to Jodie Foster:

> Over the past seven months I've left you dozens of poems, letters and love messages in the faint hope that you could develop an interest in me. Although we talked on the phone a couple of times I never had the nerve to simply approach you and introduce myself.
>
> . . . the reason I'm going ahead with this attempt now is because I cannot wait any longer to impress you. I've got to do something now to make you understand in no uncertain terms that I am doing all of this for your sake. By sacrificing my freedom and possibly my life, I hope to change your mind about me. This letter is being written an hour before I leave for the Hilton Hotel.
>
> Jodie, I am asking you to please look into your heart and at least give me a chance with this historical deed to gain your respect and love.
>
> I love you forever.
>
> John Hinckley

What a way to wow the ladies! Hinckley left the note in his room and went downstairs to catch a cab to the Hilton. At the hotel, he milled around outside among a group of people hoping to catch a glimpse of the President.

After the President's speech, several reporters ran out of the hotel, cutting in front of the onlookers for better access to President Reagan. Hinckley held his ground, ending up among the pack of news people. President Reagan emerged from the hotel at 2:25 P.M., smiling and waving to the crowd. When a reporter shouted a question, the President's press secretary, James Brady, approached him to answer.

Hinckley pulled his gun, crouched into a combat stance, and emptied the revolver at the President. He fired all six shots in less than nine seconds. The first shot hit Brady in his forehead. The second hit Washington police officer Thomas Delahanty in the neck. Secret Service agent Timothy McCarthy stepped between President Reagan and Hinckley and took the third bullet in his chest. The fourth and sixth shots missed everyone, but the fifth ricocheted off the presidential limo, striking President Reagan's chest. In the excitement, the President didn't even realize he'd been shot. Secret Service agents whisked him to the limousine and sped off to the White House.

John Hinckley was still squeezing the trigger even though the gun was empty while Secret Service agents, police officers, and bystanders piled on him. One bystander tried to choke the gunman, but a Secret Service agent intervened. Authorities shoved Hinckley into a car and took him from the scene.

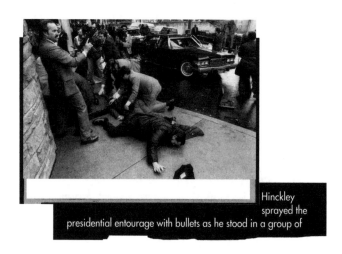

Hinckley sprayed the presidential entourage with bullets as he stood in a group of

Meanwhile, President Reagan was on the floor of the presidential limousine with Secret Service agent Jerry Parr on top of him for protection. Reagan felt a sharp pain in his chest and told Parr to get off. It wasn't until then that Parr noticed a trickle of blood at the corner of the President's mouth. Then there was more blood as the President started to cough. Parr instructed the driver to head to nearby George Washington University Hospital.

Reagan was having trouble breathing, and the pain steadily increased, but he insisted on walking himself into the hospital. He passed out as soon as he made it through the doors. A nurse found the bullet wound after they stripped off the President's shirt and examined his body. The bullet had punctured Reagan's left lung, causing his chest to fill with blood. Doctors suctioned out three and a half quarts of blood, which they replaced via transfusions. They operated immediately, finding the bullet just an inch from the President's heart.

President Ronald Reagan was a tough old bird and took the injury in stride. When the first lady arrived at the hospital, the President quipped, "Honey, I forgot to duck."

John Hinckley was charged with the attempted assassination of the president of the United States. After a forty-two-day trial, a jury of his peers found him not guilty by reason of insanity. He was institutionalized because of his mental illness. He remains so as of this writing.

Yes! I remember her. She was great!
—John Kennedy, to a staffer who showed
him a snapshot of an unnamed woman
sunbathing in the nude.

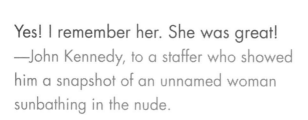

PART TWO

Sex *at the* Chief Executive Level

I'm not going to take any sleazy questions like that
from CNN. – George H.W. Bush, responding to a
reporter's question about rumors of an affair between
Bush and his longtime aide, Jennifer Fitzgerald.

PRESIDENTIAL SEX SCANDALS ARE AS American as miniature golf. From George Washington to Bill Clinton, and who knows how far beyond, our presidents have proved a fact the electorate sometimes forgets—they're human. And, as such, Chief Executive of the United States or not, they'll act on natural human instincts and urges just like the rest of us.

Some may point to the "higher standard of conduct" we expect from our elected officials. Others may argue that the scandals are simply Mother Nature at work, thus unavoidable. One might consider changing social mores in determining what qualifies as "scandalous." Whatever, you'll find no judgments here, just the facts as they've been reported through American history. Whether or not sexual dalliance at the chief executive level is scandalous, decide for yourself.

Politics is supposed to be the second oldest profession. I have come to realize that it bears a very close resemblance to the first. —Ronald Reagan

President George Washington

1

"Father" of Our Country

George Washington

GEORGE WASHINGTON TOLD THE TRUTH about cutting down a cherry tree, and he was equally honest when he wrote, "When once the woman has tempted us and we have tasted the forbidden fruit, there is no such thing as checking our appetites, whatever the consequences may be."

How Washington Proposed.

Said Washington somewhat abashed. Dear Martha, will you be
The mother of your country, love, this land of liberty?

Although he was smitten with Sally Fairfax, George Washington proposed to Martha Curtis, who became the "mother" of our country.

An observation that begs the question: Did George cheat on Martha? The answer depends on what account you want to believe. The "Stallion of the Potomac," as some friends called him, had a shaky beginning in matters of the heart.

Tall, slender, and handsome, the soft-spoken Washington pursued a number of young women—none of whom wanted anything to do with him. Successful in his career and heir to a small farm, George concluded he was doomed to a life of failure at romance. Then he met Sally.

Sarah "Sally" Fairfax swept George off his feet when he was sixteen and she eighteen. The two indulged in a flirtatious relationship for years. But, there was a small detail standing in their way— Sally was already married. Wed in fact to George's close friend and

An International Custody Battle

WHILE ON A VISIT TO THE COLONIES, BRITISH subject George Gale fell in love with a young widow from Virginia. The young mother of three from her previous marriage was ecstatic when George proposed. The couple married and George and Mildred Gale returned to live in George's native England. But family life didn't last long for the Gales, ending when Mildred died in childbirth shortly after the relocation. Mildred's will bequeathed George her money and made Mr. Gale guardian of her two boys, Lawrence and Augustine. The boys attended a British boarding school and were well on their way to becoming proper English gentlemen when their deceased father's family sent word they were disputing Mildred's will. A custody battle ensued.

After years of international litigation, a court finally ruled the boys be returned to be raised by blood relatives in Virginia. The ruling had an unknown but dramatic effect on world history.

Mildred Gale's first husband's name was Lawrence Washington. Their son, Augustine, returned to Virginia, grew up, married, and eventually had three sons of his own. He named his oldest son "George," after his stepfather. That boy, of course, turned out to be the Father of our Country, George Washington. All because of a trans-Atlantic custody battle. ✪

neighbor, George William Fairfax. In spite of the situation, Sally and George maintained their liaison for as long as seven years—even after George became engaged to Martha Custis, the richest widow in Virginia.

Historical gossip on the father of our country's love life varies. Some historians contend George and Sally's relationship never crossed the boundaries of flirtation. Others, like Wilson Miles Cary, Sally's descendant and biographer, claim the pair did the deed. Most agree, however, that once George and Martha married, the future President took his vows seriously and ended whatever physical relationship he and Sally had enjoyed.

No one knows for sure if George was stepping out on Martha after they married. Fortunately for George, "independent counsels" had not been invented yet.

2

"Brown Sugar—How Come You Taste So Good?"

Thomas Jefferson

IT IS WELL KNOWN THAT THE MAN, WHOM it delighteth the people to honor, keeps and for many years has kept, as his concubine, one of his slaves. Her name is Sally. The name of her eldest son is Tom. His features are said to bear a striking though sable resemblance to those of the president himself. The boy is ten or twelve years of age. His mother went to France in the same vessel with Mr. Jefferson and his two daughters. The delicacy of this arrangement must strike every portion of common sensibility.

President Thomas Jefferson

What a sublime pattern for an American ambassador to place before the eyes of two young ladies! . . . By this wench Sally, our president has had several children. There is not an individual in the neighborhood of Charleston who does not believe the story, and not a few who know it . . . . Mute! Mute! Mute! Yes very Mute!

Will all those republican printers of biographical information be upon this point."

—*James Thompson Callender, the Richmond Recorder, September 1, 1802*

Other than on a few minor details Mr. Callender's account is believed by many to be true. This much we know: Sally Hemings was born a slave around 1773 to Elizabeth "Betty" Hemings. It is rumored that Sally's father was her owner, Thomas Jefferson's father-in-law John Wayles. If true, Jefferson's wife, Martha, was Sally Hemings' half-sister. Jefferson took ownership of Sally as part of his wife's inheritance when Wayles died, approximately two years after his marriage to Martha.

Martha died in 1783, leaving Thomas Jefferson the freedom to return to public service. By 1785 he departed to France as America's foreign minister. Later that year, Sally Hemings was selected to accompany Jefferson's daughter Polly to France to join her father.

At fourteen years old, Sally arrived in France and was described as "decidedly good looking, beautiful, radiant, lovely and intelligent with long straight hair down her back." The fetching young beauty found an admirer in forty-two-year-old Jefferson, who apparently acted on his interest sometime the next year. By the time Sally returned to Virginia in 1789, she was noticeably pregnant. Her first child was born in late 1789 or early 1790, when Sally was seventeen. Sally's son Madison Hemings, her third child, claimed his mother became Thomas Jefferson's lover in Paris, and the affair continued after their return to Virginia until Jefferson's death in

1826. Madison also maintained Thomas was the father of all seven of Sally's children—a claim disputed by some even today.

In recent years, the Jefferson/Hemings relationship has been raised by those hoping to prove the presidential paternity of Hemings' descendants. Some biographers suggest Peter Carr, Jefferson's nephew, was the more likely father. A retired University of Virginia pathologist, Eugene A. Foster, conducted DNA studies on descendants of Hemings and Carr. DNA was collected from a descendant of Jefferson's paternal uncle Field because Thomas and Martha never produced any male children.

Nature magazine published the conclusions of the study, which showed Eston Hemings was Thomas Jefferson's son. The study also proved Peter Carr could not have been the father because the DNA on the Y chromosome did not match.

Modern science in an age-old controversy.

Jefferson's other sexual exploits include an on-going affair with Betsy Walker, the wife of his neighbor and long-time friend John Walker. He also spent time in Paris in the company of at least two women other than Sally Hemings—Maria Cosway and Angelica Schuyler Church. Perhaps the most scandalous sex rumor came in the final years of Jefferson's presidency, in 1808, when Federalist newspapers reported the President had a tryst with a politically motivated Dolly Madison. As the story goes, Mrs. Madison, wife of presidential hopeful James Madison, agreed to service the sitting Chief Executive in return for his endorsement and support of her husband. Tom contended the scenario was incredible, and Dolly claimed she would never invite a man into her bedroom unless he "was entitled by age and long acquaintance." Interestingly, neither party ever specifically denied that the story was true.

Jefferson vs. Gideon, King James, et. al

EVEN THOUGH THOMAS JEFFERSON CONSIDERED himself a God-fearing man, he took issue with many of the interpretations written in the gospels of Matthew, Mark, Luke, and John. Jefferson considered Jesus a philosopher and explained the difference between Jesus' philosophy and his own, "I am a materialist; he takes the side of spiritualism."

To reconcile himself with the New Testament, Jefferson rewrote parts of the Gospel, creating his own version, known today as the Jefferson Bible. The Jesus of the Jefferson Bible does not perform miracles. Nor does he proclaim himself the Son of God. Jefferson's Jesus doesn't ascend into heaven after crucifixion and death on the cross. Jefferson thought these ideas were added to Gospel text through "stupidity" or "roguery." In the Jefferson Bible, Jesus is portrayed as a spiritual and prayerful man, but simply a man.

Writing at night during his first term as President, Jefferson kept his "Gospel" secret to prevent public controversy. "I not only write nothing on religion," he told a friend, "I rarely permit myself to speak of it."

During his lifetime, Thomas Jefferson never revealed his altered version of the Bible. The Jefferson Bible wasn't published until seventy-five years after the President's death. ✪

3

Hard as Hickory

"OLD HICKORY," IT SEEMS, SPORTED MORE presidential wood than just his nickname, albeit with a stern price to be paid by those inclined to make issue of the fact.

President Andrew Jackson

ANDREW JACKSON.

Rachel Jackson

Young Andy Jackson met pretty twenty-one-year-old Rachel Donelson Robards at her mother's boarding house in Tennessee, where attorney Jackson stayed while performing a stint as federal prosecutor for the Tennessee Territory. Rachel was staying with her widowed mother, having been sent from her home in Kentucky by her husband, Lewis Robards, who made unfounded accusations about infidelity. Rachel had married Robards in 1785, though the relationship was always tumultuous. Robards was insanely jealous of his wife's attention. An avid cheater himself, Lewis frequently accused Rachel of fooling around behind his back. Robard's most recent tirade ended with Rachel being shipped to Tennessee.

Andrew and Rachel fell in love. The romance didn't go unnoticed by Lewis Robards, who moved Rachel back to Kentucky and challenged Jackson to a fistfight. When Andrew countered with an upgrade to an offer of a duel, Robards backed down. The abuse continued until Jackson himself traveled to Kentucky and took Rachel back to Tennessee.

By 1790 Lewis Robards hadn't given up on his missing spouse. He began rumbling about retrieving his wife from Jackson's arms in

Tennessee—using force, if necessary. Mrs. Robards and Mr. Jackson took the threat seriously and relocated to Natchez, Mississippi, to avoid Rachel's imminent abduction. Lewis responded by filing for divorce in Kentucky, claiming his wayward bride had "eloped with another man."

Word of the divorce reached Natchez by August 1791, and twenty-four-year-olds Andrew and Rachel were married. Problem was, a Kentucky court had already reviewed Robards's petition and summarily dismissed it on the grounds it was unfounded. At that moment Andrew became an adulterer, Rachel a bigamist, and Lewis the cuckolded husband.

When Lewis discovered his status, he promptly re-filed for divorce on the grounds of adultery. The divorce became final in September of 1793, and the Jacksons "re-married" on January 18, 1794, in Nashville, Tennessee.

The unseemly situation stayed buried for over thirty-five years until Jackson's political opponents exposed Andrew and Rachel's long-dead skeleton and used it to question Rachel's moral values shortly before Jackson's first presidential campaign. Embarrassed but, as always, staunch in his views, Jackson tried to protect his wife from the mudslinging by hiding the scandal.

But, as with all political dirt, the whirlwind of negative press hit the streets of Nashville and blew into Rachel Jackson's hands. Accusations of bigamy startled Rachel's weak heart. She died of a heart attack in December of 1828, three months before Andrew was inaugurated as president. The president-elect told funeral attendees, "In the presence of this dear saint, I can and do forgive all my enemies. But those vile wretches who have slandered her must look to God for mercy."

Did a presidential sex scandal ruin Andrew Jackson's bid for the White House? Obviously not, but it may have sent him to the Oval Office a widower.

Petticoats and Pistols

ANDREW JACKSON GRIEVED FOR HIS LOST RACHEL throughout his first term as president—when he wasn't simmering in bitter hostility against the political foes he blamed for her death. But despite his loneliness and depression, his first term was not without titillating scandal. Known as the Petticoat Affair, the scandal concerned Jackson's friend and Secretary of War, John Henry Eaton, a former senator from Tennessee.

Eaton has violated social propriety by marrying Margaret "Peggy" O'Neale only eight months after the death of her husband, John Timberlake, who slit his own throat while at sea. Timberlake was a purser in the Navy and had battled financial problems. Eaton had been a close friend of the couple and had been seen frequently with Margaret in social settings while Timberlake was at sea.

Washington's gossip grapevine hummed about the buxom, saucy Margaret and the older Eaton, speculating that they had been having an affair, which might have contributed to Timberlake's suicide. Even those who didn't believe that rumor were still upset that the couple had married when Margaret should have been in mourning.

But Margaret was a vivacious iconoclast, know throughout Washington because her father owned the Franklin House, an inn where many congressmen lived and dined during their time in the city. She was known as flirtatious, quick-witted, and outspoken, hardly a paradigm of gentility like the typical wives of Washington society. And those other wives hated her. Vice President John Calhoun and his wife were particularly snarky, ignoring Margaret at White House dinners and receptions.

Andrew Jackson, always quick to take offense (and even more so after Rachel's death), stood by his friend Eaton and the new, if never blushing, bride. The affair disrupted more than high-society gatherings. It leaked into nearly every aspect of political life and consumed vast amounts of the new administration's time. The presidential cabinet was split by the scandal and some members quit or were dismissed. Members of both political parties called for Eaton's dismissal, but Jackson refused to consider such a move. He lashed out at anyone—even his niece, Emily, who acted as the first lady—who opposed or were in any way rude to the Eatons.

The ever-wily Martin Van Buren, by supporting the couple, raised his political stock with Jackson, leading to his selection as vice-president on the next Democratic ticket and, eventually, to his winning the presidency. Van Buren came up with the idea of having the entire Cabinet resign, himself included, which would allow Eaton to leave gracefully. Jackson agreed and made Eaton governor of the Florida Territory and later the ambassador to Spain. Eaton and Jackson eventually had a falling out and were never close friends again. When Eaton died in 1856, his wealthy fifty-nine-year-old widow took up with her granddaughter's nineteen-year-old dance teacher. The unlikely pair married, though the young lothario ended up running off to Europe with the granddaughter—and all of Margaret's money. She died years later, impoverished. ✪

Slingin' Mud in 1828

THE PRESIDENTIAL CAMPAIGN OF 1828 STILL REIGNS as one of the nastiest in American history. The Republican incumbent, John Quincy Adams, and his longtime rival, Democrat Andrew Jackson, leveled accusations and sparred with words like a pair of MMA fighters. Jackson supporters continued to gripe about the 1824 election they claimed Adams stole in a corrupt backdoor deal Adams made with Henry Clay. They also accused Adams of being a fornicating monarchist who engaged in premarital sex with his wife, who they claimed was the illegitimate child of unwed parents. The Jacksonian press even went so far as to accuse Adams of pimping for Czar Alexander I of Russia because Adams had recommended a young American nursemaid to the czar's family. Apparently, the charge had some basis in fact judging from letters the young lady had written her family describing the czar's sexual antics. The accusers also pegged President Adams as a man of poor morals for installing a billiards table in the White House and swimming nude in the Potomac River.

John Q's people got down and dirty too. They claimed that Andrew Jackson was the bastard son of a prostitute mother and a mixed-race father named Jack. They said Jackson had a brother who was a slave. They trashed Jackson's military record, making him appear a butcher on the battlefield. But the hardest thing for Andy to take was the charge he was a home-wrecker and adulterer who lured his wife Rachel from her first husband. They called Rachel an adulteress and bigamist, charges that were technically true since she hadn't received a valid divorce before marrying Jackson in the Natchez Territory in 1791, even though the couple remarried in 1794 when the matter was straightened out. In the end Old Hickory took the White House in 1828, but not until both sides suffered enough abuse to leave both candidates battered and bruised. ✪

James Buchanan

Engraved by permission from the original in the possession of J.C.Buttre, Esq.

President James Buchanann

100

4

A Gay Old Time with the Bachelor President

AN AIR OF MYSTERY SURROUNDED THE suicide of twenty-three-year-old Anne Coleman in December of 1819. Why would the brown-eyed, raven-haired beauty, the daughter of one of the richest men in Pennsylvania, cash in her own chips? She was, after all, engaged to a handsome and promising young attorney, James Buchanan, whose aspirations would surely fulfill any woman's dreams. But Anne reconsidered the engagement in the midst of rumors of philandering on James's part and tales that the future president was marrying for money—not love.

So Anne broke off the engagement. Buchanan tried to change her mind, albeit unsuccessfully. Anne's true reasons for dumping James went to the grave with her. We do know she became depressed after breaking off the engagement. Wanting to get away, she left her home in Lancaster to visit a sister in Philadelphia. Upon arrival in the City of Brotherly Love, Anne made the acquaintance of local judge Thomas Kittera, who later described the encounter:

> At noon yesterday I met this young lady on the street, in the vigor of health, and but a few hours after, her friends were mourning her death. She had been engaged to be married, and some unpleasant misunderstanding occurring, the match was broken off. This circumstance was preying on her mind. In the afternoon she was laboring under a fit of hysterics. . . . After night she was attacked with strong hysterical convulsions, which induced the family to send for physicians, who thought this would soon go off, as it did. But her pulse gradually weakened until midnight, when she died.

One doctor on the scene described the death as ". . . the first instance he ever knew of hysteria producing death." Although the official cause of death remains a mystery, word at the time was that Anne committed suicide by overdosing on drugs. James mourned her death for the rest of his life. He started his political career with a successful run for Congress in 1820 as a "distraction from his great grief."

Some say Buchanan became "the Bachelor President" in 1857 after taking a vow to never marry in light of Anne's death. But there may have been another reason for Buchanan's perpetual single life. It involves a different side of the fifteenth president, a darker side he himself may have denied and repressed. And it involved a man, not a woman.

Around the time James Buchanan went to Congress in 1820, Alabama also sent a freshman to the House of Representatives in one William Rufus King. The pair became longtime friends, and in 1852 King ran on the Democratic Party's ticket for the White House. He was elected to serve as Vice President for President Franklin Pierce.

As roommates and best friends for twenty-three years, Buchanan and King, according to some, shared more than living space. Evidence exists that they were homosexual. They seemed inseparable and spent so much time together in Washington they were often referred to in and out of the press as "the Siamese twins." In 1844 Tennessee Congressman Aaron Brown marked "Confidential" on a letter to Mrs. James K. Polk when he wrote:

> Mr. Buchanan looks gloomy and dissatisfied and so did his better half until a little private flattery and a certain newspaper puff which you doubtless noticed, excited hopes that getting a divorce she might set up again in the world to some tolerable advantage. Since which casual events, which she has taken for real and permanent overtures, Aunt Fancy may now be seen every day, trigged out

Gone—and Forgotten

PRESIDENT MARTIN VAN BUREN MARRIED HANNAH Hoes, his childhood sweetheart, on February 21, 1807. According to historians, the marriage was successful, and the couple had four sons. Hannah died of tuberculosis on February 5, 1819, when she was only thirty-five years old, and Martin never remarried. Strangely, in his autobiography, he never mentions Hannah—not once. ✪

in her best clothes and smirking about in hopes of securing better terms than with her former companion. . . . But
I have done with metaphor and in words. . . .

It seems that Brown is referring to King as Buchanan's "better
half," "Aunt Fancy," "Mrs. B.," and Buchanan's "wife," coupled with
talk of "a divorce." It appears that the Congressman was informing
Mrs. Polk of the couple's breakup and commenting on King's search
for a new mate.

William King may also have insinuated his sexual preference
when, in an 1844 letter to Buchanan penned while he was minister
to France, he wrote:

> I am selfish enough to hope you will not be able to pro-
> cure an associate who will cause you to feel no regret at
> our separation. For myself, I shall feel lonely in the midst
> of Paris, for here I shall have no Friend with whom I can
> commune as with my own thoughts.

Did young Anne Coleman end her life at her fiancé's revelation
he was gay? Perhaps we'll never know for sure. James Buchanan
indicated he recorded the true reason for his and Anne's breakup in
sealed documents he deposited in a New York bank years after her
death. However, when he died, Buchanan's executors discovered
a note attached to the documents expressing James's wish they be
destroyed unopened. That's exactly what they did.

Luckily for James Buchanan, neither Anne Coleman's prema-
ture demise nor his apparent sexual preferences affected his political
career. Any private pain remained his own.

Skinny-Dipping in the Potomac

BY MOST ACCOUNTS, JOHN QUINCY ADAMS WAS ONE of the most straight-laced individuals to ever serve as president. But one of his favorite routines was to take a daily stroll to the Potomac River, strip naked, and go skinny-dipping.

Rumors around the nation's Capital about the President's outdoor buff-baths abounded. Thurlow Weed, a New York politician, wanted to check it out for himself. He spied Adams on his stroll before daybreak and watched as the President stripped along the way, tied his clothes in a bundle, and took the plunge. Thurlow noted that the President had the aura of a nudist: "He seemed as much at ease in that element as on Terra Firma."

On another sunrise swim, Adams had a servant row him across the Potomac in an old boat. The President planned on swimming back, but a squall blew up, sinking the boat and dumping both men in the water. They managed to swim back to the other side, but the servant lost his clothes and the fifty-eight-year-old Adams was exhausted by the effort. Adams let the servant use his clothes and got in some "naked basking on the bank" while he waited for the man to return with a carriage. The President took the "humiliating lesson" in stride, though. And even though his wife called it "altogether ridiculous," the early morning naked swims continued.

Newspaper journalist Anne Royall, who had been unable to get an interview with Adams, knew about his early-morning routine and went to the river one morning. When he was back-stroking in the buff, she took his clothes and sat on them and said she wouldn't give them back until he agreed to an interview. He did—making her the first female journalist to interview a president. ✪

5

Three-Ways and Ho's on the Road to the White House

RUMORS OF PRESIDENT JAMES GARFIELD'S philandering ways circulated widely while he occupied the White House. One claimed he celebrated his presidential election by visiting a New Orleans brothel in 1880. Even though James and his wife, Lucretia, called the rumors "nothing more nor less than an infamous lie," the facts show that James had a habit of adultery.

Technically, his first fling didn't qualify as an extramarital affair because he wasn't married at the time, merely engaged. James met his future wife Lucretia, whom he called "Crete," in 1849 and the two became engaged in 1854. As a senior at New York's Williams College in 1855, James spent the Thanksgiving holiday near school at the home of Mrs. Maria Learned in Poestenkill. It was Maria—who seemed to have designs on young Garfield herself—who introduced James to Rebecca Jane "Rancie" Selleck, a petite twenty-four-year-old described as "elegant, sensuous and witty."

The three friends met frequently in what seemed, at first, to be a platonic relationship. But Maria's eye for James expressed itself by way of encouragement to Rancie to take her attraction for Garfield to a sexual level. The two consummated the affair one night in December of 1855 in Garfield's room in the Learned house, which he had deemed the "the prophet's chamber."

By all appearances, Garfield and Rancie continued their sexual romps until November of 1858, when the wayward fiancé made good on his pledge to marry fair Lucretia. The newlyweds did not go on a honeymoon.

James Garfield may have the distinction of being the first future president to cheat on his wife. Although it's possible George Washington did, and Thomas Jefferson certainly did have affairs with married women, Garfield did for sure. In October of 1862, shortly after a stint with the Union Army in the Civil War and on a visit to New York, Garfield briefly carried on with Mrs. Lucia Gilbert Calhoun, an eighteen-year-old reporter for the *New York Times*. Not many details are known about the affair. By now Crete had resigned herself to James's philandering. But trust him she did not. In 1867, Garfield again visited Lucia in New York, presumably to retrieve love letters. His troubled wife wrote him in obviously mistrustful tones:

> Somehow I cannot but feel that to her at least you would
> compromise your love for me were you voluntarily to go

into her presence. And for her too I believe it would be better to let the fire of such lawless passion burn itself out unfed and unnoticed. James, I should not blame my own heart if it lost all faith in you. I hope it may not . . . but I shall not be forever telling you I love you when there is evidently no more desire for it on your part than present manifestations indicate.

President James Garfield

Robbing the Cradle

PRESIDENTS JOHN TYLER AND BENJAMIN HARRISON were not known to be unfaithful to their wives. In fact, they were widowers. But both got busy during their presidential years. Tyler lost his wife, Letitia, in 1843, while he was in the White House. The couple had been married for nearly thirty years and had raised seven children. Letitia suffered a stroke in 1839 and was an invalid during Tyler's presidency, rarely appearing in public. When she died, he immediately began courting the beautiful Julia Gardiner, who was twenty-four years old, thirty years younger than Tyler. The couple had seven children of their own. Tyler's years in the White House weren't happy ones, but he seemed to enjoy life afterward quite a bit.

Benjamin Harrison married a woman twenty-five years younger than himself after his first wife, Caroline, died from tuberculosis shortly before Harrison was defeated for a second term. Mary Scott Lord Dimmick was Caroline's niece and, at thirty-seven, younger than both of Harrison's children. Mary had lived at the White House during Harrison's term, assisting the first lady, whose health was poor for a long time. There were no rumors of hanky-panky between the President and his wife's niece, and the couple waited until 1895 to become formally engaged, nearly three years after Caroline's death. Nevertheless, Harrison's children were furious at their father and refused to attend the wedding or to acknowledge Mary as their father's wife. Benjamin and Mary had one child, Elizabeth, born in 1897. ✪

President Grover Cleveland

6

Who's Your Daddy?

Grover Cleveland

IT WAS 1884, LONG BEFORE DNA TESTING took all the fun out of determining paternity, and relatively-new-to-politics Grover Cleveland had just secured the Democratic Party's nomination for a run at the White House. And so the mudslinging began with allegations that the candidate was a fornicator and the father of an illegitimate ten-year-old boy. Maria Crofts Halpin, a widow from New Jersey who hooked up with Cleveland in Buffalo, NY, claimed Grover was the father of her son, Oscar Folsom Cleveland. The affair, which Cleveland never denied, occurred in 1873 to 1874 as Grover (or "Big

Steve" to his friends) was finishing his tenure as Buffalo's sheriff and entering private law practice. At the age of thirty-five, Maria had just left two children in New Jersey to start anew in northern New York.

Republicans fueled the scandalous fires in hopes of carrying New York State and winning the presidency for their candidate, James G. Blaine. Newspapers across the nation ran editorials and cartoons inferring that such a sexually promiscuous scoundrel was unfit to serve as President. The Republicans even paid the National Music Company of Chicago to print and distribute a song entitled "Ma! Ma! Where's My Pa?" Influential Republican clergyman Henry Ward Beecher was among some who saw through the hypocrisy, saying, "If every New Yorker who had broken the seventh commandment were to vote for Cleveland, he would carry the state by a large majority."

"Ma! Ma! Where's My Pa?"

Even though Cleveland never denied he was Oscar's father, the boy's true paternity wasn't certain because Ms. Halpin was boinking not only Grover, but some of his friends as well. But Cleveland manned-up and took responsibility for little Oscar, even letting him use his last name. Maria tried to pressure Cleveland into marriage, but he resisted. She then took to the bottle and fell into the embraces of alcoholism. Because of her chronic drunkenness, Cleveland had Maria committed to an asylum and arranged to pay for Oscar's keep in an orphanage. When Maria was released, Cleveland paid to start a new business for her in Niagara Falls. Maria ultimately sued for custody of Oscar in 1876, but was denied by the courts. Frustrated, she kidnapped the boy, but was located by Cleveland three months later. Grover paid Maria to give up parental rights and leave town. She moved to New Rochelle and found a husband. Oscar was

Hanging Out in Buffalo

A SURPRISING NUMBER OF U.S. PRESIDENTS HAD "unusual" jobs before they entered politics. Teddy Roosevelt was a cowboy. Harry Truman earned a living as a haberdasher. And George W. Bush owned a major league baseball team, the Texas Rangers. Grover Cleveland was an executioner.

Cleveland started in the workforce as a lawyer. He entered politics in 1870, when he was elected sheriff of Erie County, New York. As the chief county law enforcement official, Sheriff Cleveland assumed the duty of executioner of those condemned to death within his jurisdiction. For years, the executioner job was delegated to a deputy, Jake Emerick, who hanged so many convicts (remember, it was the 1870s) he acquired the nickname "Hangman Emerick," a title he and his family found disturbing.

In 1872, a man named Jack Morrissey was found guilty of murdering his mother and received a death sentence. But Morrissey was well known in Erie County, and the circumstances of his mother's death generated a lot of sympathy for the condemned man within the community, who believed he deserved a pardon. When attempts at a pardon failed, and Deputy Emerick already stressed about "pulling the hatch," Grover Cleveland announced that he would carry out the execution himself because he didn't feel right having a subordinate do the dirty work that came with his office.

When Jack Morrissey went to the gallows, Cleveland was there, standing behind a screen separated by twenty feet from the doomed convict. At the appointed time, the future president pulled the lever, releasing the trapdoor that sent Jack Morrissey to meet his maker. Friends said Cleveland was sick for days over what he had done. In the 1884 presidential election, opponents mocked the candidate as "the Buffalo Hangman," but in performing the duty of his elected office, dirty as the task might have been, Grover Cleveland built the foundation of a record of public integrity that eventually helped take him to the White House. ✪

adopted by a wealthy New York couple. Later in life, he became a respected physician.

Ironically, during the presidential election, the Democratic staff learned that Republican candidate Blaine had a secret of his own. Apparently, he had married in a rather rushed shotgun wedding. The newlywed's first child was born a mere three months later. Blaine explained the biologically impossible error by saying he had actually married twice—once in a private ceremony held six months prior to the public occasion.

In the end, it wasn't sexual impropriety that decided the election. Most credit Blaine's defeat in 1884 to Republican supporter Reverend S.D. Burchard, who spoke to a group of five hundred ministers at a rally for Blaine in New York. He described the Democratic Party to the attendees, and the press, as "the party of Rum, Romanism, and Rebellion." New York's large Roman Catholic population, especially the Irish, took umbrage at the remark and turned out in large numbers to vote, eventually delivering Cleveland's victory in New York by a mere 1,150 ballots. In the Democratic victory of electoral votes 219-182, New York's thirty-six votes tipped the scales.

The Dems couldn't resist adding a new line to "Ma! Ma! Where's My Pa?" with the finish "Gone to the White House, Ha! Ha! Ha!"

7

Woody at the White House

WOODROW WILSON'S SEXUAL INDISCRE-
tion occurred while he was president—of Prince-
ton University in 1907. He took a much-needed
vacation, upon doctor's orders, to the island of
Bermuda. His wife, Ellen, didn't accompany the
future chief executive as she suffered her own
medical issues. While alone in Bermuda, Wilson met Mary Peck, the wife of a wealthy Massachusetts industrialist, who was dealing with a
bout of depression on the pink sandy shores.

(left) President Woodrow Wilson
(below) Ellen Wilson

The two became quick friends. The affair heated up either on Wilson's second visit to Bermuda in 1908 or during a visit to Peck's New York apartment in 1909 after she and her husband, Thomas, separated. Mary and Woodrow wrote each other frequently and met whenever possible at the apartment. Their affair ended in 1910, shortly before Wilson was elected governor of New Jersey, but when the Pecks filed for divorce in 1912 the specter of infidelity raised its head as rumors started to fly that Thomas Peck was using some of Wilson's letters as proof of Mary's adultery.

Governor Wilson's political foes found out about his love letters to a married woman, but thought better of exposing them because, as Theodore Roosevelt pointed out, "You can't cast a man as a Ro-

Woodrow never dipped into that well again.

meo who looks and acts so much like an apothecary's clerk." Wilson even prepared a press release admitting "a passage of folly and gross impertinence," but didn't ever have a need to use it. Despite the lack of public disclosure, Ellen Wilson found out about the affair. A forgiving soul, Ellen let bygones be bygones with Woodrow and Mary Peck, even to the point of playing host to Mrs. Peck or staying at Peck's New York apartment. But, Woodrow never dipped into that well again. He last saw Mary after Ellen's death in 1915.

Freud on Woody

THE ONLY U.S. PRESIDENT TO EVER BE PSYCHO-
analyzed by the famous Sigmund Freud was Woodrow Wilson. Well, sort of. Wilson had already passed on to the big White House in the sky, but Freud found the former president so fascinating he co-authored a book applying psychoanalysis techniques to remembrances of Woodrow Wilson. When he finished, Freud found the work so controversial he didn't want it published until Wilson's widow also passed away. The book wasn't released until 1966, more than twenty-five years after Freud's own death.

Freud co-wrote the book with former Wilson advisor William Bullitt. In it, Freud contends that President Wilson suffered from severe personality defects that prevented him from succeeding at creating a lasting peace following World War I. (Wilson failed at efforts to persuade the U.S. Senate to ratify the Treaty of Versailles or to enter the League of Nations, largely due to his own intransigence.) Professor Freud states that Wilson displayed signs of being a neurotic who suffered from a domineering father and an overprotective mother, and who lacked the masculine will to carry out his policies. Freud also thought Mr. Wilson suffered from a savior complex and needed to be worshiped to satisfy the demands of his superego. He also described Colonel Edward House, one of the President's most trusted advisors, as Wilson's "chief love object."

Critics trashed the book, a response Freud probably would have taken in stride. "What progress we are making," he once said. "In the Middle Ages they would have burned me. Now they are content with burning my books." ✪

8

The Ladies' Man
from Ohio

Warren G. Harding

THE SEVENTH ANNIVERSARY

I love you more than all the world

Possession wholly imploring

Mid passion I am oftime whirled

Oftimes admire—adoring

Oh God! If only fate would give

Us privilege to love and live!

> —Warren G. Harding to his lover Carrie Phillips in a
> letter dated Christmas, 1915

(above) President Warren G. Harding.
(right) Florence, or Flossie, was a tough
old bird who seemed to care more
about being first lady than about her
husband's philandering.

Ohio has spawned more than its share of controversial politicians, perhaps none more than the twenty-ninth president of the United States, Warren G. Harding. Born in 1865 in Blooming Grove, Ohio, to prominent country physician George Harding and schoolteacher Phoebe Dickerson Harding, young Warren grew up in the small nearby town of Marion, the eldest of eight children. A graduate of Ohio Central College, Harding found his first real job as editor of the *Marion Times Star* newspaper, a daily he co-owned with his father, who maintained his medical practice across the hall in the same building in downtown Marion.

Young Harding was handsome and charming. He prospered on the local scene and found himself popular with the ladies. He caught the eye of divorcee Florence "Flossie" DeWolfe, an heiress-apparent of the wealthiest family in town. She was five years older than Harding, already once divorced with a son by her ex-common law husband, and he soon became the object of her desires.

Neither beautiful nor charming, Flossie seemed an odd choice for the dashing Warren, though her money and her ambitions for him must have had a certain appeal. They married in 1891 over the staunch objections of Florence's father Amos Kling, a business rival of Warren's who, according to Harding biographer John Dean, tried to defame his son-in-law by claiming his ancestry was African-American. (This rumor would surface throughout Harding's political career despite proof to the contrary.)

The Marion Republican found his way into politics in 1895 when he ran for, and lost, the position of auditor of traditionally Democratic Marion County.

Not one to be denied, Harding again ran for political office with the help of the shrewd and savvy Flossie, who he had dubbed the "Duchess" because of her arrogant demeanor and quick temper, which she apparently inherited from her father. This time Harding managed to be elected to a senate seat in the Ohio General assembly in 1899. A stint as lieutenant governor followed in 1904 until

1905, when he took a break from politics to tend to his wife's failing health.

But Warren became restless in private life. Between 1905 and 1910, Amos Kling and Warren had reconciled their differences, and Florence's health improved. Harding made another bid for the Ohio governor's mansion in 1910 but lost. He then seemed to lose interest in politics and focused on his personal interests. But Amos Kling died in 1913, leaving the Hardings financially comfortable and with renewed political ambitions. The next year he ran for the U.S. Senate and won. In 1920, Harding was elected by popular vote to the highest office in the land. The man from Marion's presidential legacy began.

In a little more than three years as president, he was accused of a number of improprieties, most famously for the "Teapot Dome Scandal," which involved Harding's secretary of the interior, Albert Fall, who sold access to oil on federal land. This scandal was eclipsed by a series of sexual indiscretions with a pair of fellow Ohioans from Warren's beloved hometown of Marion.

Carrie Phillips, nine years younger than Warren, was a pretty strawberry-blonde schoolteacher and the wife of his longtime friend, Jim Phillips. In 1904, tragedy struck the Phillips household when the couple's four-year-old son, Jim Jr., suddenly died. Mr. Phillips

Warren G. with his wife, Florence, whom he dubbed "The Duchess."

became quite distraught and decided to take a sabbatical, at the suggestion of his friend, Mr. Harding, at a Michigan sanatorium where Warren had spent time years before while suffering from nervous exhaustion.

During the mister's absence, Warren called on Mrs. Phillips, presumably to console her. Warren found Carrie alone in her bedroom where the "comfort" he offered became sexual. Mr. Harding found the "love of his life" that day and began an affair that lasted on and off for fifteen years.

With their spouses apparently oblivious, Warren and Carrie seemed to take every opportunity for adulterous playtime. When they were apart, they corresponded in what certainly qualifies as "lust letters" as much as "love letters."

"I love you garbed, but naked more," Harding wrote to his sweet mistress. In another letter, published in a 1976 edition of the *Washington Post*, he cooed, "There is one engulfing, enthralling rule of love, the song of your whole being which is a bit sweeter—Oh Warren! Oh Warren—when your body quivers with divine paroxysms and your soul hovers for flight with mine." Harding even tried his hand at poetry: "Carrie, take me panting to your heaving breast."

Although Warren seemed quite satisfied with the arrangement, Carrie occasionally demanded that he leave his wife to marry her. In mortal fear of "the Duchess," and of ruining his political career, Warren steadfastly refused. By 1914, ten years into the affair, Florence Harding finally figured out what was going on and threatened Warren with divorce. He was able to talk her out of it, while still managing to continue the soiree for six more years. Jim Phillips didn't find out about his wife's infidelity until 1920, and probably not until Carrie told him. Although Carrie promised Warren she was destroying the love letters he wrote through the years, by 1920, and the presidential election, she was embittered and threatened to expose their adultery by providing the sordid pages, which she had kept, to the press.

Candidate Harding responded by buying her a new Cadillac and offering $5,000 a year "in order to avoid disgrace in the public eye, to escape ruin in the eyes of those who have trusted me in public life."

When his offer appeared to fall short of her requirements, a nervous Republican National Committee got involved. They sent an emissary to Jim and Carrie Phillips, eventually getting them to agree to a payment of $20,000 and a trip around the world with an extended stay in the Orient plus $2,000 per month as long as Harding remained in office. Jim and Carrie graciously accepted the offer.

Like many others, the Phillips' lost their financial security during the Great Depression. Jim Phillips succumbed to the bottle and died broke in 1939. Carrie developed a reputation as an eccentric until senility forced her into a nursing home, where she died in 1960. An attorney found Warren's love letters in her estate in 1963. According to Wesley O. Haygood, author of *Presidential Sex*, the letters are now in the possession of the Library of Congress and remain sealed under court order until July 29, 2014.

Years younger than her lover, Nan Britton chased after Warren Harding from an early age, eventually bearing his daughter. Nan seemed to be the consummate "other woman."

Amazingly, Warren Harding's extended affair with Carrie Phillips wasn't his only indiscretion, nor was it the most notorious. For several overlapping years and well into his presidency, Warren kept company with a young woman twenty years his junior, another Marion resident named Nan Britton. Nan was born in 1896 to a local physician and his schoolteacher wife who lived in the same neighborhood as the Hardings. By the time she was fourteen, Nan was already infatuated with Mr. Harding after seeing his picture on a Republican campaign poster in Marion. She apparently proclaimed her affection for Harding to anyone willing to listen.

The crush remained innocent enough until 1917 when Nan wrote to the Ohio senator upon her graduation from secretarial school inquiring about a letter of reference. More than happy to oblige, Senator Harding arranged a meeting with his young admirer to discuss her future. In May of that year, the two met in a reception room at the Manhattan Hotel in New York City. Small talk soon turned into discussion of Nan's early declarations of affection for Mr. Harding. It wasn't long before Nan confided to the senator that she still held those same feelings. Seemingly not surprised by the revelation, Warren suggested the two go up to his room where they could continue the discussion "without interruptions or annoyances."

"We had scarcely closed the door behind us when we shared our first kiss, it seemed sweetly appropriate," Britton later wrote, "I shall never forget how Mr. Harding kept saying, after each kiss, 'God! . . . God Nan!' in high diminuendo, nor how he pleaded in tense voice, 'Oh, dearie, tell me it isn't hateful to you to have me kiss you!' And as I kissed him back I thought that he surpassed even my gladdest dreams of him."

Although Nan claims their first encounter didn't go beyond the kisses, by July of 1917 she and Warren enjoyed regular sexual intimacies. Nan was rather naïve when it came to such matters, and so it was in 1919—on a trip to Senator Harding's Washington, D.C., office, where the two made love—that Britton says Harding's only child was conceived. In July of 1919, Elizabeth Ann was born. Mother and baby, albeit separately, attended the Republican national convention the following August to watch Warren G. Harding win the Republican nomination for the office of president of the United States. They would not see each other again until after the election.

In her book *The President's Daughter*, Nan wrote of her first visit to President Harding in June of 1921:

> Whereupon he introduced me to the one place where, he said, he thought we might share kisses in safety. This was a small closet in the anteroom, evidently a place for hats and coats, but entirely empty most of the times we used it, for we repaired there many times during the course of my visits to the White House, and in the darkness of a space not more than five feet square the President of the United States and his adoring sweetheart made love.

On at least one occasion Nan and President Harding were having sex in the White House closet when the Duchess, apparently tipped off by a Secret Service agent, tried to catch the two in the act. The president's bodyguard blocked the door, however, forcing the enraged Mrs. Harding to circle the mansion and enter through another door. By the time she got there the President's man had managed to get Nan out a back door and Florence found only a flustered Warren sitting sheepishly at his desk.

By January 1923 the president worried about the effect a scandal involving a mistress and illegitimate child would have on his re-election. He told Nan his fears and added, according to Britton, that he would provide for mother and child as long as they lived. It was the last time they met. Harding died later that year. No provisions were left for Nan Britton or her daughter. Britton published *The President's Daughter* in 1927. The book tells her story and the story of the "love child" she shared with Warren Harding. Although she was destitute by then and probably needed the money, Britton explained her motivation for writing the book as ". . . the need for legal and social recognition and protection of all children in these United States born out of wedlock."

President Warren Harding died on August 2, 1923, only 882 days into his first term. His legacy of scandal, however, lives on despite Harding biographer John W. Dean's (no stranger himself to presidential scandal as a convicted conspirator in the Watergate investigation) book about Harding's life. In the book, Dean asserts: "While in office, Harding had his critics, as do all presidents, but few presidents have experienced the unrequited attacks and reprisals visited on one of the most kindly men ever to occupy the Oval Office. It hasn't been pretty." Dean describes his work as "not to challenge or catalogue those who have gotten it wrong about Harding, only to get it right."

Right or wrong, President Harding's death precluded him from defending himself against any allegation. Even the circumstances of his demise became fodder for scandal. By the time he was laid to rest at the Warren Harding Memorial in his hometown of Marion, theories and speculation raged about his sudden death.

By today's standards, Warren Harding's lifestyle made him the perfect candidate for a heart attack. He lived the "high life" in pre-prohibition America with a fat-filled diet complimented by regular tobacco and alcohol consumption. Exercise for the president consisted mostly of rounds of golf and twice-weekly poker games, accompanied by the occasional off-the-cuff love trysts. Natural causes seemed a perfectly plausible explanation, but one of Harding's attending doctors in San Francisco offered another possibility. Dr. Joel Boone, according to his diaries and memoirs as mentioned in crimelibrary.com, felt a physician's negligence may have contributed to Harding's demise. According to Boone, Harding's primary physician, Dr. Charles Sawyer, attributed the President's symptoms of angina to indigestion compounded with ptomaine poisoning from "a mess of King Crabs drenched in butter" which Sawyer treated with "powerful purgatives" that eventually sent the patient into cardiac arrest. Of four physicians present, only Sawyer seemed to believe the "official" cause of death—stroke—to be true. The other three, particularly Boone, believed it was a heart attack, prompted by the powerful purgatives provided by Dr. Sawyer. According to crimelibrary.com, the other three physicians most likely agreed with Sawyer's diagnosis to protect his reputation from being damaged for malpractice involving the President of the United States.

A doctor's error is only one of four scandalous theories surrounding Warren Harding's unexpected death. Others surmised the President committed suicide because of the political damage occurring from the Teapot Dome scandal. Crimelibrary.com takes the suicide theory a couple of steps further, exploring the possibility that Harding was murdered—perhaps for political reasons by those involved in Teapot Dome, or by the Duchess with the dual motives of protecting his reputation and as a form of revenge for her husband's adulterous ways.

Has history been unfair in its treatment of Warren Harding? Is a president's sex life a private matter not to be scrutinized by the public? Perhaps the answers lie in Dean's conclusion to **Warren G. Harding** in which he quotes a poem read by Harding's Secretary of State Charles Evans Hughes at a memorial eulogy delivered to the joint session of Congress on February 28, 1924:

> Let who has felt compute the strain
> Of struggle with abuses strong,
> The doubtful course, the helpless pain
> Of seeing best intents go wrong.
> We, who look on with critic eyes,
> Exempt from actions crucial test,
> Human ourselves, at least are wise
> In honoring one who did his best.

9

FDR and the Secretary of Sex

PERHAPS IT WAS BECAUSE ELEANOR MAY have regarded sex as a marital obligation to be endured. Or maybe it happened as Franklin's way of affirming his manhood through sexual activity after the polio virus wreaked havoc on his body. No matter the reasons, Franklin Delano Roosevelt's mention of "no symptoms of impotentia coeundi" in his doc's examination report were affirmed by the thirty-second president time and again.

Lucy Page Mercer was Eleanor Roosevelt's social secretary in 1913 and 1914. It was likely then that the attractive twenty-two-year-old made the acquaintance of a rising star in national politics in FDR. In the summer of 1916, when Roosevelt was assistant secretary of the Navy, Franklin and Lucy began an almost thirty-year affair. Eleanor had taken the children to the family summerhouse at Campobello in Canada. Lucy became Franklin's escort to social functions and on overnight trips.

The following year Mr. Roosevelt remained in the summer heat of Washington while the Mrs. and kids escaped for Campobello. Eleanor was becoming suspicious, but not to the point of confrontation. Franklin continued seeing Lucy and took her freely around Washington's social elite. The political social circles hummed with

Lucy Mercer wasn't FDR's ONLY outside love account.

gossip about the pair, but Eleanor was either overly trusting or blissfully ignorant.

Then, in September of 1918 when an ailing Franklin returned from Europe with a case of double pneumonia, Eleanor decided to unpack his luggage. There she found Franklin's mail, which included love letters proving her husband's involvement with her former secretary. Years later, Eleanor described her feelings at discovery of the affair, telling author J.P. Lash, "The bottom dropped out of my own particular world and I faced myself, my surroundings, my world, honestly for the first time. I really grew up that year."

Devastated, Eleanor confronted her husband in the presence of his mother, Sara, who immediately threatened to cut her son's finances. Eleanor offered him a divorce, but in those days the only

Girlfriends

IN LATE JUNE OF 1932, ELEANOR ROOSEVELT
met an Associated Press reporter named Lorena Hickok.
Ms. Hickok was assigned to cover the nominee's wife at
the Democratic National Convention in Chicago. The future first lady and
the reporter became quick friends. Hickok, a lesbian, eventually quit her
job and moved into the White House in 1941. She lived in the executive
mansion for the next four years.

The first lady nicknamed Lorena "Hick." Although Hick had her own
room, she often stayed in Eleanor's room, according to one of the White
House maids. The arrangement disturbed FDR, who was once overheard
shouting, "I want that woman kept out of this house!" There is speculation
that the two women shared a sexual relationship, but Elliott Roosevelt, one
of Eleanor's sons, thought it unlikely.

Eleanor's feelings are well documented in the more than two thousand
letters she wrote Lorena over their thirty-year relationship. In those letters,
which are stored at the Roosevelt Presidential Library in Hyde Park, New
York, Eleanor often wrote passages revealing strong affection. For example, on March 7, 1933, Lorena's fortieth birthday, Eleanor wrote:

> Hick darling, All day I've thought of you & another birthday I will be
> with you. . . . Oh! I want to put my arms around you. I ache to hold
> you close. Your ring is a great comfort. I look at it and think she does
> love me or I wouldn't be wearing it!

In another 1933 note, Eleanor wrote Hick:

> Good Night, dear one. I want to put my arms around you and kiss
> you at the corner of your mouth. And in a little more than a week
> now—I shall."

You be the judge. ✪

grounds for such action in New York was adultery, and a scandal would end Roosevelt's budding political aspirations.

Franklin and Lucy promised to end the relationship.

They lied.

The affair continued until the day FDR died. In the meantime, Eleanor became more independent and detached from Franklin and remained so for the rest of his life.

In 1920, Lucy Mercer married a wealthy fifty-eight-year-old widower named Winthrop Rutherfurd. Rutherfurd had six children and Lucy's new family's demands lessened the time she could spend with Roosevelt. But they still saw each other occasionally and wrote letters. At his first inauguration, a presidential limousine was sent for Mrs. Rutherfurd, who watched the ceremony from the car. She attended all the Roosevelt inaugurations in the same fashion. After Winthrop's death in 1944, Lucy was a frequent guest at the White House when Eleanor was away. FDR and Lucy Mercer Rutherfurd spent time together in Warm Springs, Georgia, on the day he died. She was swiftly dispatched in an unsuccessful effort to keep Eleanor from discovering she was there.

Lucy Mercer wasn't FDR's only outside love account. In 1921, the future President started a long-term affair with Marguerite Alice "Missy" LeHand, a worker in his failed vice presidential bid in 1920. Missy started as his personal secretary shortly after his bout with polio, accompanying him to rehab sessions as well as performing clerical duties. She remained his personal secretary for nearly twenty years.

When the Roosevelts moved into the governor's mansion in 1928, FDR and Missy had adjoining rooms. Eleanor's room was down the hall. When Roosevelt moved to the White House, Missy also moved in, taking a three-room suite, though she frequently spent the night in the Chief Executive's bedroom.

She suffered a cerebral hemorrhage in 1940 and had to move out of the White House. The affair ended, and she died in 1943. In his estate, Roosevelt left nearly two million dollars to cover Missy's medical bills.

Other rumors of Roosevelt's sexual prowess circled around DC toward the end of his life. One involved Princess Martha of Norway, who spent World War II in the United States and had total access to the President and his residences. There is no hard evidence of anything more than public flirting in the relationship, but gossips of the day speculated about more private flirtation. Another unsubstantiated affair stems from a claim from Dorothy Schiff, the publisher of the *New York Post*, who claimed she bedded Roosevelt in a year-long affair from 1944 to 1945.

For a guy who walked with crutches, Mr. Roosevelt definitely got around.

10

I (Really) Like Ike!

Dwight Eisenhower

IT WAS LIKE AN EXPLOSION. WE WERE suddenly in each other's arms. His kisses absolutely unraveled me. Hungry, strong, demanding. And I responded every bit as passionately. He stopped, took my face between his hands. "Goddamnit," he said, "I love you."

President Dwight D. Eisenhower

We were breathing as if we had run up a dozen flights of stairs. God must have been watching over us, because no one came bursting into the office. It was lover's luck, but we both came to our senses, remembering how Tex had walked in earlier that day. Ike had lipstick smudges on his face. I started scrubbing at them frantically with my handkerchief, worrying—what if someone comes in?

Ike put his hands on my shoulders. "We have to be very careful," he said. "I don't want you to be hurt. I don't want people to gossip about you. God, I wish things were different."

"I think things are wonderful." I whispered. I knew what he was talking about. I understood the problem. And I did not believe for a moment that love conquers all. But still everything was wonderful. I did not expect anything to be easy. But I was not one to deny love. I could see no reason to deny it. This is part of the business of living in this special dimension, in our case the tunnel of war, where all your feelings, all your energies are absorbed by one great purpose. Your world is different from that of other people, divorced from the world outside the tunnel. What was important here and now was that there was love—pulsating, irrepressible love."

—*Kay Summersby Morgan, Past Forgetting: My Love Affair With Dwight D. Eisenhower*

Dwight Eisenhower met thirty-one-year-old Kay Summersby, twenty years his junior, on a ten-day, fact-finding trip to London during World War II in May 1942. An exuberant, brunette Irish lass with sparkling blue eyes, Kay had been assigned as Ike's driver to show him and General Mark Clark around war-torn London. Ike and Kay immediately had chemistry, and he asked her to be his driver should he ever return—which he did, just a month later.

(above) Mamie Eisenhower played the role of stoic wife well. (right) Mamie and Ike watching television together.

They began an intimate relationship that continued for the duration of the war. The press reported on Ike's daily life, often including photos of him with his lovely driver. Mamie Eisenhower noticed the attention, but Ike reassured her he "liked some and was intrigued by others" but he had not been unfaithful.

Kay accompanied him on a trip to Algiers, and rumors of a sexual liaison grew. Kay dismissed the notion to friends, reminding them that she was happily engaged to Richard Arnold, an army colonel. But that relationship ended when Arnold was killed while inspecting a minefield.

The relationship bumped up to the sexual level, sort of, in the fall of 1943. Ike had been in meetings in the States for twelve days and hooked up with Kay immediately upon his return to London. The passion fizzled, however, because, according to Kay, Ike was impotent. Ike told Kay he'd "try my damnedest," but subsequent attempts at sex met with the same disappointing results.

A letter from Eisenhower to General George Marshall proves Ike's love for Kay. In it he states his intention to divorce Mamie to marry Kay. The letter ended up in Eisenhower's personnel file at the Pentagon. Later, President Harry Truman saw the correspondence and had it destroyed for propriety's sake.

After the war, Eisenhower returned to Washington, leaving Kay behind in London. After her discharge from the army, Kay moved to New York City, where Eisenhower had become the president of Columbia University. But chances for the pair had passed. Ike eventually admitted, "It's impossible. There's nothing I can do." They were history.

Kay authored two books about her relationship with Eisenhower. *Eisenhower Was My Boss*, the first, makes no mention of the personal relationship they shared. In 1976, a year after Kay's death, *Past Forgetting: My Love Affair With Dwight D. Eisenhower* was published.

Jacqueline Bouvier Kennedy was America's ideal modern twentieth-century wife. She went to great lengths to ignore JFK's philandering and protect his presidential image.

11

"Where're the Broads?"

John F. Kennedy

THE NEWLY INAUGURATED PRESIDENT JOHN Fitzgerald "Jack" Kennedy asked the question in the title upon arrival at a late-night post-swearing-in-ceremony party at the Georgetown residence of columnist Joe Alsop. JFK was unarguably the horniest individual to ever occupy the Oval Office—which puts him high in the running for horniest individual ever. Indeed, the "broads" were there on January 20, 1961, and JFK took full advantage of the situation.

Jack's sexual prowess began when he lost his virginity to a prostitute in a Harlem brothel at the age of seventeen. Following his father Joe's advice to "get laid as often as possible," he never looked back. Chronicling Kennedy's sexual exploits is a formidable, maybe impossible, task. It's likely there are hundreds of encounters that will never come to light. Kennedy insider Ted Sorenson once joked with Kennedy, "This administration [Kennedy's] is going to do for sex what the last one [Eisenhower's] did for golf." The president responded with, "You mean nineteen holes in one day?"

Popular movie stars, burlesque queens, expensive call girls, common prostitutes, White House staffers, secretaries, stewardesses, socialites, campaign workers, political groupies, and "friends of friends," Jack boned them all. A mere sampling includes:

Inga Arvad (aka "Inga Binga")

In 1941 Jack was serving a tour of duty for the Navy in Washington, where his sister, Kathleen, introduced him to twenty-eight-year-old former Miss Denmark Inga Arvad, whom Jack nicknamed "Inga Binga." The blue-eyed blond was gorgeous and sophisticated. She also knew her way around the bedroom and had the sexual appetite to manage twenty-four-year-old Jack Kennedy. Even though Inga was married at the time, she and Jack decided to share her Washington apartment.

Inga was an actress in Germany prior to coming to America. She also worked as a correspondent, even interviewing Adolf Hitler and other Nazi brass. Hitler was so smitten by the young beauty he insisted she visit whenever she was in Berlin. Because of her Teutonic affiliations, the FBI suspected Inga Binga of being a spy. They consequently bugged her apartment, secretly recording her sexual romps with young Jack. The Navy tried to end the relationship by transferring Kennedy to a post in Charleston, South Carolina, but Jack couldn't give up Inga and continued the liaison—and the Feds continued the wiretap. FBI director J. Edgar Hoover found great

A PROVOCATIVE FILM FOR ADULTS!

The party **GIRLS** of the **POLITICAL** jungle...The **RAW** truth of **SEX, BLACKMAIL, SLANDER** and **POWER!**

JERRY BLAINE
presents

THE ★★★ CANDIDATE

"my bed is not for sale!"

STARRING MAMIE VAN DOREN / JUNE WILKINSON

TED KNIGHT / ERIC MASON / RACHEL ROMEN

and the PARTY GIRLS

Produced by MAURICE DUKE · Directed by ROBERT ANGUS · Screenplay by JOYCE ANN MILLER · QUENTON VALE

A *Cosnat* PRODUCTION

D. 401

Not everyone ignored President Kennedy's obvious cocksmanship. As this promo shows, the movie The Candidate exploited rumors of steamy sex in the nation's capital.

leverage in the recordings of JFK and Inga Binga "engaging in sexual intercourse on a number of occasions."

By February of 1942, Papa Joe Kennedy got word to Jack of the bugs and phone taps. Jack dumped Inga Binga forthwith. The duo spoke on the phone and saw each other occasionally, but the affair ended. At one point Inga turned up pregnant, but paternity was unclear. Inga's son, Ronald McCoy, said his mother once told him Jack Kennedy was his father.

Strippers and Ho's

Jack enjoyed way more than a tease with two famous burlesque queens in Tempest Storm and Blaze Starr. The future president met voluptuous Tempest Storm in 1955 when she was performing at Washington's Casino Royale Theatre. The amply endowed, six-foot stripper hooked up with Jack whenever she was in town. Apparently Ms. Storm was as talented in bed as she was onstage (she was boinking Elvis Presley around the same time). Tempest fondly described Mr. Kennedy as "almost insatiable in bed."

"Jack the John" managed to bang amateurs and pros alike. One professional he tapped was legendary stripper Tempest Storm.

Jack's liaison with Blaze Starr only lasted about twenty minutes. In 1960 Blaze and her fiancé, Louisiana Governor Earl Long, were attending a campaign party at a New Orleans hotel. The striking future president managed to lure Starr to a closet in the next room. Blaze contends that while the two were having sex Jack regaled her with the story of Warren G. Harding and Nan Britton's similar tryst in the White House coat closet.

In 1963, *New York Journal-American* reporters Don Frasca and James Horan published an article revealing that one of the "biggest names in American politics" who held a "very high elected office" enjoyed numerous sexual encounters with British model and actress Suzy Chang in New York City during 1960 and 1961. Frasca and Horan also claimed they had proof that the same elected official had group sex with nineteen-year-old London prostitute Maria Novotny and two of her call-girl friends. Novotny told investigators from the FBI and Scotland Yard thatshe did indeed meet Kennedy when she was nineteen in December of 1960 at a party hosted by singer Vic Damone at a New York hotel. Novotny said Jack's brother-in-law, actor Peter Lawford, made the introduction. Shortly after they met, Maria and Jack retired to an empty bedroom for casual sex. Maria also told investigators that Lawford requested she do something "a bit more interesting for the president." Maria and two other working girls met "Jack the John" in a Manhattan apartment dressed as nurses and provided sexual services to their executive patient. The newspaper left Kennedy's name out of the article. Then-U.S. Attorney General Bobby Kennedy promptly threatened to smack the paper with an antitrust lawsuit should it print any more stories. None ever went to print.

Joan Lundberg

Jack was visiting his sister Pat and her husband, Peter Lawford, in southern California in 1956 when he met Joan Lundberg, a divorced mother of two, in a Santa Monica nightclub. Lundberg caught Jack's attention, and soon the pair paired up at a late-night party at the Lawfords' home. A three-year affair ensued. According to Joan, the two could appear discreet when together because Joan's appearance resembled his sister Pat's, which would cause people to assume Jack and Joan were related. Joan became a kept woman with Jack serving as sugar daddy to all of her needs, even to the point of offering to pay $400 for an abortion when it became a necessity.

Joan said Jack, "loved threesomes—himself and two girls. He was also a voyeur," implying perhaps he liked to watch the girls pleasure each other. Jack often confided in Joan his fear that as he was busy cheating, his wife Jackie was playing similar games. After four years, Lundberg and Kennedy broke off the affair immediately after Jack won the Democratic presidential nomination. Their parting was amicable.

Pamela Turnure

Senator Jack Kennedy met twenty-year-old Pamela Turnure when he was forty. She was brunette with blue-green eyes and a fair complexion. Some said Pam reminded them of Jackie Kennedy in the way she looked and spoke. Pam eventually became Senator Kennedy's receptionist and sex partner. Living within driving distance, the young secretary was the frequent recipient of Jack's late-night booty calls at her apartment in Georgetown. The visits didn't go unnoticed. Ms. Turnure's landlords, the Katers, took offense at the cavorting. They even recorded and photographed Jack's tomcat behavior, which they offered to the FBI and the press, who largely ignored them. After Jack was elected President, Mrs. Kater expressed her displeasure at the affair by picketing the White House carrying a sign that read, "Do you want an Adulterer in the White House?"

When Kennedy was elected president, Pam took a job as the first lady's press secretary. Pam had no qualifications for the job, but her office was in the White House, and she was always available to service the President when he had the urge. Jackie likely knew about the affair. Some surmise she wanted Jack and Pam close so she could better monitor their behavior. Or perhaps she hoped her husband would tire of the young secretary, which may have happened. "There are two naked girls in the room, but I'm sitting here reading the *Wall Street Journal*. Does that mean I'm getting old?" Jack once asked a friend over the telephone.

Florence Pritchett Smith

The Palm Beach police chief didn't see the new president and Florence Smith swimming, per se, in Florence's pool. Jack had managed to ditch the FBI, the Secret Service, and the chief on a trip to the Sunshine State, sneaking away to visit Mrs. Smith who was, by then, an old friend. No stranger to giving people the slip, Jack had managed to attend a private skinny-dipping party with Florence until the frantic authorities caught up.

Florence Pritchett Smith was the fashion editor for the *New York Journal-American*. She was also the wife of E. T. Smith, Dwight Eisenhower's U.S. Ambassador to Cuba. With brown hair and eyes, Florence was smoking hot. In 1957 and 1958, Jack managed to make trips to Cuba for some time alone with Florence. He also traveled to Miami or Palm Beach whenever she was in town.

Priscilla Weir and Jill Cowan

The randy young president dipped more than his toe into the White House secretarial pool. That's where "Fiddle and Faddle" got their chance to lay the most powerful man in the world. Also known as Priscilla Weir and Jill Cowan, the nicknames came courtesy of the Secret Service—as code names for sensitive radio communications. Both in their early twenties and attractive, Priscilla was a blonde and Jill a brunette. They applied for their jobs at the White House together, wearing identical dresses.

Priscilla and Jill didn't have any secretarial skills, but it seems skills in the bedroom more than qualified the pair to make frequent trips with the President to places like Nassau, Palm Beach, and Yo-semite National Park. Fiddle and Faddle were usually housed near the President's private quarters so they could be summoned at any hour for late night "work." Since Jack was fond of ménage-a-trois sex, it's likely the President, Fiddle, and Faddle had White House three-ways. LBJ's press secretary George Reedy once confirmed girl-boy-girl liaisons and added the trio was also fond of swimming nude in the White House pool.

Judy Campbell

Jack Kennedy met Judith "Judy" Eileen Katherine Immoor Campbell during the presidential campaign of 1960 at the Sands Hotel in Las Vegas. Jack took a break to drop in on Frank Sinatra at the Sands and catch his show. Sinatra introduced the candidate to the black-haired, blue-eyed Judy, who later wrote about the meeting: "He looked so handsome in his pinstripe suit. Those strong white teeth and smiling Irish eyes." The candidate was also impressed and seemed determined to get to know Ms. Campbell much better.

After a month of frequent phone calls and red-rose deliveries, Jack arranged a meeting with Judy at New York's Plaza Hotel. It was March 7, 1960, the evening before the New Hampshire primary. The two talked over a bottle of Jack Daniel's and then had sex. According to Judy, no mention of the primary was ever made. The first

Ever Ready

JOHN KENNEDY WAS THE FIRST BOY SCOUT TO become president. When it came to "broads," he certainly took the Scout motto to heart and was always "prepared." ✪

encounter concluded with the delivery of a dozen red roses to Judy's room the next morning. The card read, "Thinking of you," signed only with the initial "J."

About a month later, Judy journeyed to the Kennedys' Georgetown home. Jackie, who was pregnant, was in Florida at the time. Jack and Judy dined alone, and after dinner Jack offered his guest a tour of the house. The tour ended in the master bedroom where Judy noticed twin beds. Judy went into the bathroom to undress and when she came out she found her host naked and eagerly waiting. Judy later said she felt awkward about making love in Jackie and Jack's bed, but her attraction overcame her conscience.

Judy and Jack saw each other intermittently, but the relationship took a different twist right after the first day of the 1960 Democratic National Convention in Los Angeles on July 11. Jack and Judy were alone in Peter Lawford's suite at the Beverly Hilton Hotel. After drinks and conversation, Jack asked Judy to accompany him to the bedroom. She was surprised to find a tall, thin young woman in her late twenties waiting for them in the room. The woman went into the bathroom and closed the door. Jack suggested to Judy that the three of them go to bed together. Judy angrily left. She didn't stay upset for long, however, and the affair continued through the rest of the campaign and into Kennedy's early presidency.

During the summer of 1961, Judy called the President frequently. She claims she made booty calls to the White House more than twenty times that summer. According to White House phone logs, Judy called Jack over seventy times between 1961 and 1962. Probably not coincidentally, the last call came on March 22, 1962, just hours after President Kennedy met with FBI director J. Edgar Hoover at the presidential mansion. Although it's likely Jack already knew, Hoover probably warned him of Judy's relationship with Chicago crime boss Sam "Momo" Giacana, and the dangers the affiliation could cause politically. In fact, Jack and Giacana had already met, via Judy, and Giacana had helped Kennedy defeat Hubert Humphrey in the 1960 primary campaign, using mob money to get the vote in West Virginia.

Despite the lack of physical records, Judy claims she carried on with Kennedy at least as late as June 1962, meeting him for sex in the White House family's private quarters. But the grind of secrecy and deception began to wear on the affair, and the two drifted apart. Although Judy had no way of knowing, this was about the time Jack had found another sex playmate in Mary Pinchot Meyer.

Mary Pinchot Meyer

Mary Pinchot Meyer met Jack Kennedy while he was a student at Choate. They saw each other into college while she attended Vassar and he was a student at Harvard. But the pair didn't hook up until early 1962 when they were re-introduced at a party by Mary's brother-in-law, *Washington Post* executive editor Benjamin Bradlee. A divorcee since 1959, Mary lived a bohemian lifestyle around Georgetown, maintaining a comfortable art studio and showing moderate success with her work. Shortly after reuniting, the two began their sexual romp in January of 1962 at the White House. Mary and the President continued the affair until his death in November 1963.

On various occasions, Mary brought drugs into the White House for she and Jack to use during their lovemaking sessions. A week before a White House conference on drugs, Jack and Mary smoked marijuana inside a White House closet. After sharing a couple of joints, Jack joked about being too high to "push the button" in case "the Russians drop a bomb." Mary reportedly also introduced JFK to LSD.

Mary was murdered in October 1964, while jogging along a towpath by the Potomac River. She was shot in the head and the chest. There was an arrest in the case, but no conviction due to lack of evidence. The case remains unsolved. According to Benjamin Bradlee, he discovered his sister-in-law's diary and turned it over

An early sexual conquest for JFK was Hollywood glamour star Gene Tierney. When the actress realized the relationship would end in little more than a notch on Jack's bedpost, she bailed from the romance.

to CIA counter-intelligence Chief James Angleton, who claimed he destroyed it to protect Mary's two young sons.

Gene Tierney

In 1946, young Jack Kennedy took a vacation to Los Angeles, hell-bent on "knocking a name." He found a name in glamorous actress Gene Tierney. Gene's marriage to Oleg Cassini was on the

Playboy at Large

EVERYBODY SEEMED SURPRISED TO SEE THE normally straight-laced Jimmy Carter in the pages of Playboy magazine during the 1976 presidential campaign. It was well known that the Democratic candidate was a devout Christian, and the mere risk of tarnishing that image in a major men's publication seemed out of character.

But according to Mr. Carter, the interview went well. The reporter thanked him and turned off the tape recorder, and then asked Jimmy "off the record":

> Governor, there is still one thing that really concerns me. You are a farmer, living in a small town, who has pledged never to lie to the American people. You claim to be a born-again Christian. The citizens of our country and other public officials are not perfect. How will you be able to relate to them, when you consider yourself so much better than they are?"

Carter's response, though not well received by some, made it into print. Most found it to be refreshingly honest and concise:

> Because I'm just human and I'm tempted and Christ set some almost impossible standards for us. The Bible says, 'Thou shalt not commit adultery.' Christ said, I tell you that anyone who looks on a woman with lust has in his heart already committed adultery. I've looked on a lot of women with lust. I've committed adultery in my heart many times. . . . This is something that God recognizes, that I will do and have done, and God forgives me for it. But that doesn't mean that I condemn someone who not only looks on a woman with lust but who leaves his wife and shacks up with somebody out of wedlock. Christ says, don't consider yourself better than someone else because one guy screws a whole bunch of women while the other guy is loyal to his wife. The

guy who's loyal to his wife ought not to be condescending or proud because of the relative degree of sinfulness.

"I lusted in my heart" became a catch-phrase of the era, in part because of its unlikely source, the courtly Jimmy Carter, who went on to win the presidential election. ✪

rocks, and Jack swooped into an affair that lasted for almost a year. Gene once spoke of her affair with Kennedy: "I was deeply in love with John, and I would have married him in a minute if he had been able to ask me. But Rose made it clear that no good Irish Catholic would marry a divorced woman."

Jayne Mansfield

When Jayne Mansfield met an untimely demise, her publicist, Raymond Strait, continued to ride the gravy train and wrote *Jayne Mansfield and the American Fifties* and *Here They Are: Jayne Mansfield*. In his books, Strait claims Jayne confessed to a sporadic, multiyear sexual affair with Jack Kennedy that began at the Democratic National Convention in 1960. Strait claims one encounter occurred at Jack's West Hollywood, apartment even though Ms. Mansfield was eight months pregnant at the time.

Angie Dickinson

Even through years of rumors, glamorous actress Angie Dickinson has never denied or confirmed an affair with Jack Kennedy. She's said little about Kennedy except to express her affection and admiration for him. If there was a hook-up, it was most likely during 1962, when President Kennedy was also busy boinking Marilyn Monroe, Jayne Mansfield, Judith Campbell, and Mary Pinchot Meyer.

Marilyn Monroe

Actor and Kennedy in-law Peter Lawford introduced JFK to Marilyn Monroe in 1954 at a Hollywood party thrown by agent Charles Feldman. Marilyn and Jack flirted, and as Marilyn exited the event with her husband, Joe DiMaggio, she managed to slip a note with her phone number to JFK. Marilyn divorced DiMaggio in 1955. She later wed famous playwright Arthur Miller.

With Peter Lawford's assistance, Jack and Marilyn carried on a relationship well into his presidency. Once, disguised as Lawford's secretary, Marilyn caught a ride on Air Force One. She told close friends that Kennedy was "less than inspired" in the sack, concluding that he "made love like an adolescent." But she also daydreamed about becoming Mrs. JFK—the first lady. The affair eventually became more obvious to the White House staff and Secret Service, who often found the President and the blonde bombshell in compromising positions.

Several of the President's cabinet members protested when they discovered Ms. Monroe was scheduled to perform at the President's forty-fifth birthday party in May 1962, which was also a Democratic fundraiser. The first lady was so upset she didn't even attend. Marilyn delivered a rendition of "Happy Birthday" that was almost as sexually charged as her form-fitting gown. JFK, who probably would have enjoyed the provocative birthday wishes more in a private setting, didn't take kindly to the public forum. The pair spent what was likely their last night together. Shortly after his birthday party, Kennedy stopped taking Marilyn's calls. Marilyn took the dumping hard, making threats to go public with the affair. JFK sent brother Bobby to handle the actress. Apparently Bobby achieved in this modest task, perhaps by starting his own affair with Marilyn. Everything ended on August 4, 1962, when Marilyn was found dead in her Hollywood home of an overdose of sleeping pills.

12

Walking Tall from Texas

LBJ ALWAYS SEEMED PROUD OF HIS womanizing ways. He had sex, inside and outside the White House, with secretaries, aides, and just about any other woman who would agree. Johnson was quoted as saying he had "more women by accident than Kennedy did on purpose," a formidable claim. Johnson enjoyed bragging about his sexual appetites and prowess in true "Texas fashion." Despite his promiscuity, LBJ had at least two long-lasting affairs.

(above) President Lyndon Johnson.
(right) Lady Bird Johnson. LBJ's
marriage to Lady Bird may have been
for money more than love.

The first lasted nearly thirty years from 1938 until 1965 with a lady named Alice Glass. Alice was the mistress and later the wife of Texas millionaire Charles E. Marsh, publisher of the *Austin American Statesman* who also had newspaper interests across the nation. Lyndon and Alice first met in 1937 at Marsh's Culpepper, Virginia, estate. Alice was twenty-three years younger than Marsh and found young Johnson quite irresistible.

At one time, Alice believed Lyndon would divorce his wife to marry her, but she realized the effect a divorce would have on Lyndon's political career. So the couple settled for a long-term adulterous affair, sometimes meeting at the Mayflower Hotel in Washington, sometimes at Marsh's estate. It is unlikely the affair could have been kept secret from Lady Bird Johnson or Charles Marsh, but both seem to have resigned themselves to it.

Ironically, the liaison ended around 1965 over political disagreement. Alice opposed the Vietnam War and apparently wanted no more to do with its then-Commander In Chief. She even burned Lyndon's love letters in protest.

In 1948, twenty-three-year-old Madeleine Brown was an advertising buyer for radio in Texas. She met Johnson at a reception hosted by Austin radio station KTBC, which Johnson owned. According to Ms. Brown, shortly after another event she and LBJ hooked up at an Austin hotel for a sex session. Afterward, KTBC's station manager would act as intermediary in setting up sexual encounters for the pair. Lyndon and Madeleine would meet at different hotels in Texas anytime Johnson was there on business or making a campaign visit.

In 1950, Madeleine told Johnson she was pregnant with his child. Steven Brown was born in 1951. However, on the birth certificate Brown listed her estranged husband as the father. In 1987, Steven Brown filed suit against Lady Bird Johnson and Lyndon's estate for $10.5 million, claiming unjust denial of his inheritance and his name. The lawsuit never made it to trial, however, as it halted when Steven died of lymphatic cancer.

Trysts between LBJ and Alice Glass sometimes took place at the Mayflower Hotel in downtown Washington, which has a history of hosting illicit love affairs.

The affair ended in a dispute over Steven's paternity in 1969 at the Shamrock Hotel in Houston. Steven was over six feet tall and seemed to resemble Lyndon. Madeleine claims she tried to persuade LBJ to acknowledge being Steven's father for over two hours, but he wouldn't consider the notion because of Lady Bird and his two daughters.

Shortly after LBJ died in 1973, Texas lawyer Jerome T. Ragsdale contacted Brown to say plans had been made to continue to provide for her and Steven. Ragsdale had been providing financial support, including a house, to Madeleine since Steven's birth. In 1997, Madeleine Brown published an account of her affair with LBJ entitled *Texas in the Morning: The Love Story of Madeleine Brown and President Lyndon Baines Johnson.*

Of Zippers, Knives, and Bungholes

PRESIDENT LYNDON BAINES JOHNSON CLAIMED TO have bedded more women than even Jack Kennedy, though LBJ certainly lacked JFK's looks, charm, and sophistication. Maybe the key to his success can be found in the song by Texas band ZZ Top, who told us that "Every girl crazy 'bout a sharp-dressed man."

Johnson apparently gave a lot of thought to his clothes, at least from what we can gather from a conversation he taped with Joe Hagger of Hagger slacks. For reasons still unclear, Johnson recorded hundreds of his personal phone calls, from confidential business to ordering new pants. In the following transcript, we learn about another side of LBJ—specifically, his backside:

LBJ: Mr. Haggar?

JH: Yes, this is Joe Haggar.

LBJ: Joe, is your father the one that makes clothes?

JH: Yes, sir. We're all together.

LBJ: Uh huh. You all made me some real lightweight slacks, uh, that he just made up on his own and sent to me three or four months ago. There's a light brown and a light green, a rather soft green, a soft brown.

JH: Yes, sir.

LBJ: And they're real lightweight now, and I need about six pairs for summer wear.

JH: Yes, sir.

LBJ: I want a couple, maybe three of the light brown—kind of an almost powder color, like a powder on a ladies' face. Then there were some green and some light pair. If you had a blue in that or a black, then I'd have one blue and one black. I need about six pairs to wear around in the evening when I come in from work.

JH: Yes, sir.

LBJ: I need . . . they're about a half a inch too tight in the waist.

JH: Do you recall, sir, the exact size? I just want to make sure we get them right for you.

LBJ: No, I don't know. You all just guessed at 'em I think, some . . . wouldn't you have the measurement there?

JH: We can find it for you.

LBJ: Well I can send you a pair. I want them half an inch larger in the waist than they were before except I want two or three inches of stuff left back in there so I can take them up. I vary ten or fifteen pounds a month.

JH: All right, sir.

LBJ: So leave me at least two and a half, three inches in the back where I can let them out or take them up. And make these a half an inch bigger in the waist. And make the pockets at least an inch longer, my money, my knife, everything falls out . . . wait just a minute.

[pause]

LBJ: Now the pockets, when you sit down, everything falls out, your money, your knife, everything. So I need at least another inch in the pockets. And another thing . . . the crotch, down where your nuts hang . . . is always a little too tight, so when you make them up, give me an inch that I can let out there, uh, because they cut me, it's like riding a wire fence. These are almost, these are the best I've had anywhere in the United States.

JH: Fine.

LBJ: But, uh, when I gain a little weight they cut me under there. So, leave me, you never do have much of margin there. See if you can't leave me an inch from where the zipper . . . BUR-RRRP . . . ends, round, under my, back to my bunghole, so I can let it out there if I need to.

JH: Right.

LBJ: Now be sure you have the best zippers in them. These are good that I have. If you get those to me I would sure be grateful.

JH: Fine, now where would you like them sent, please?

LBJ: White House. ✪

13

A New Definition of Sex

BILL CLINTON HAD NUMEROUS SEXUAL partners over the years, both before and after he married Hillary Rodham. Some affairs were fleeting and some lasted for years. The single incident bringing the most attention to Bill Clinton's sexual history occurred on May 6, 1994, when a woman named Paula Corbin Jones filed an unprecedented civil suit against President Bill Clinton in U.S. district court in Little Rock, Arkansas, seeking $700,000 in damages for "willful, outrageous, and malicious conduct" at the Excelsior Hotel in Little Rock on May 8, 1991.

(above) President Bill Clinton
(right) First Lady Hillary Rodham
Clinton

Jones worked for the office of economic development for the state of Arkansas, which was hosting a conference at the Excelsior. According to Jones, she was summoned to Governor Clinton's suite, and when she walked into the room Clinton propositioned her and exposed himself to her. She says the Governor requested oral sex and, when she refused, she was dismissed with Clinton telling her to keep the matter to herself. Jones claimed she could prove the Governor flashed her by describing a "distinguishing characteristic" on his genitals. Pandora's box was opened. The following, as radio broadcaster Paul Harvey liked to say, is some of "the rest of the story."

According to a woman named Dolly Kyle Browning, in 1964 she began an affair with Bill Clinton that lasted almost thirty-three years. The two met as children at a Hot Springs, Arkansas, golf course when she was eleven and Bill was thirteen. Dolly said she was always smitten with Bill. In 1997, Browning authored a "fictional" account of the relationship entitled *Purposes of the Heart*. Lucianne Goldberg, a literary agent, arranged a six-figure advance offer if Browning would re-write the book as nonfiction. Browning turned down the offer, partly because the manuscript was written as a type of self-therapy for the sexual addiction Browning was fighting. When the book was published, the White House declined to comment.

Browning also alleged that she was approached by a tabloid newspaper to sell the story of her liaison with Clinton during the 1992 presidential campaign. She said she got word of the offer in an attempt to get direction from the candidate. Clinton allegedly asked Browning's brother, Walter Kyle, a Clinton campaign worker, to tell her if she cooperated with the reporter she would be "destroyed." At their high school reunion in 1994, Browning says Clinton tried to bury the hatchet by inviting his former classmate to move to Washington where the two could rekindle their relationship. Browning, a successful Dallas lawyer, declined the offer.

When Paula Jones filed a sexual harassment suit against Bill Clinton in 1994, Jones's lawyers subpoenaed Dolly Browning, indicating that she would confirm the "distinguishing characteristic" of Bill's penis. But the case settled out of court, negating the need for Browning's testimony.

Another lawsuit accusing Bill Clinton of sexual impropriety came after Arkansas state employee Larry Nichols was fired by then-Governor Clinton in 1990 for allegedly using state telephones to raise funds for the Nicaraguan contras. Nichols denied the allegation and countersued Clinton for defamation of character and libel. In his suit, Nichols alleged the Governor had been guilty of misconduct in office for maintaining a secret slush fund of taxpayer money he used to entertain women. Nichols cited six women in the suit, naming only five. The sixth, he said, had "become pregnant and had an abortion," thus he declined to reveal her name. The other five were Deborah Mathias, Elizabeth Ward, Susie Whiteacre, Lencola Sullivan, and Gennifer Flowers.

Flowers found Bill's suggestion

Deborah Mathias was a reporter for the *Arkansas Gazette*. She had previously worked at television station KARK with Gennifer Flowers. Flowers said she was uncertain if Clinton and Mathias had an affair, but Bill had warned Flowers about Mathias, saying she had "a big mouth."

Elizabeth Ward was a young beauty queen who won both the Miss Arkansas and Miss America crowns in 1981. According to Larry Nichols, shortly after Bill and Elizabeth met they started a heated sexual relationship. Ward said she eventually left Arkansas "because her affair with Clinton got too hot to handle." In 1992 Elizabeth Ward posed nude for Playboy magazine, prompting the Clinton campaign to issue a statement, signed by Ward, denying the affair.

Susie Whiteacre was Governor Clinton's press secretary. Nichols claimed the Governor used Arkansas State Troopers to drive the pair to various locations for sexual trysts. Whiteacre denied having a sexual relationship with Governor Clinton.

Clinton met Lencola Sullivan, Miss Arkansas, in September of 1980. The African-American beauty queen had recently placed fourth in the Miss America pageant. Nichols claimed the two hooked up the very same month. Sullivan had taken a job with KARK-TV and worked with Mathias and Flowers. But the job in Hot Springs didn't last long. Lencola suddenly moved to New York, where she had neither a job nor a place to stay. According to Nichols' lawsuit, the Clinton campaign rushed Sullivan out of Arkansas to prevent the affair from going public. Nichols also claimed Bill Clinton used taxpayer money for three trips to New York for interstate booty calls with Lencola.

Gennifer Flowers became the best known of the women named in Larry Nichols' lawsuit. Flowers claims she and Bill carried on a

"repugnant" and "too kinky."

twelve-year affair that began in 1977 while he was Arkansas attorney general. Gennifer says the affair started shortly after she interviewed Clinton for a story for KARK-TV.

Gennifer and Bill would meet for sex sessions at the Excelsior Hotel in Hot Springs or at Gennifer's apartment at the Quawpaw Towers, where the manager confirmed Clinton was a regular visitor. In December of 1977, Gennifer thought she was pregnant. When Bill provided her abortion money, she realized she would never be anything more than his mistress.

In her 1995 book *Gennifer Flowers: Passion and Betrayal*, she wrote that she and Bill would have sex as frequently as three or four times a week. She also claims Clinton liked phone sex and he introduced her to oral sex. Flowers explained that Bill researched the subject of oral sex and concluded that it didn't constitute adultery.

According to Gennifer, as the relationship progressed, so did Bill's sexual appetite. She says when she refused to let Bill tie her up he in turn asked to be tied up. He enjoyed being spanked and once requested that she use a vibrator on him. Flowers found Bill's suggestion of a ménage a trois "repugnant" and "too kinky."

Gennifer Flowers ended the affair in 1989, feeling she had met someone else whom she may want to marry. When Nichols's lawsuit was filed a year later, she began to record her telephone conversations with Clinton in case she needed to provide documentation of her story. She recorded conversations with Clinton on three occasions in 1991 and 1992.

Flowers claims that she was approached by Arkansas Republican Ron Fuller and offered $50,000 to go public with her story in October of 1991, shortly after Bill Clinton announced his presidential candidacy. She declined the offer. But the January 13, 1992, issue of the tabloid *The Star* featured a story about the five women mentioned in Larry Nichols' lawsuit. *The Star* subsequently printed another story that provided details of the Flowers-Clinton affair. Flowers then met with *The Star's* managing editor Dick Kaplan because he had told her he was going to run the story, whether she confirmed it or not. She agreed to confirm the story for between $100,000 and $150,000.

Hillary Clinton weighed in on the scandal. She claimed Gennifer Flowers fabricated the story for the money. On Super Bowl Sunday 1992, Bill and Hillary Clinton were interviewed on the CBS news show *60 Minutes*. Both Clintons acknowledged "trouble in the marriage" at some points but denied Bill had ever carried on an affair with Gennifer Flowers. Bill contended Flowers was just "a friendly acquaintance." But in his 1997 deposition in the Paula Jones suit, he admitted having a sexual affair with Flowers, though he still denied the affair lasted twelve years. After the *60 Minutes* interview aired, *The Star* arranged for Gennifer Flowers to hold a press conference at the Waldorf-Astoria Hotel in New York. At the

Gennifer Flowers posed nude for some steamy photos appearing in Penthouse Magazine after her affair with the then-president went public. The layout came complete with a no-holds-barred explicit interview.

conference, Flowers read a prepared statement and played part of one of her taped phone conversations with Bill.

She also received cash for appearing on the television show *A Current Affair*, and she mimicked Marilyn Monroe's provocative "Happy Birthday, Mr. President" song on the Comedy Channel. She appeared in the December 1992 issue of *Penthouse* magazine in a nude photo layout, in which she provided intimate details of sex with Bill, revealing, "He ate pussy like a champ!" She also used the opportunity to challenge the first lady: "I dare Hillary to bare her butt in any magazine. They don't have a page that broad."

Gennifer Flowers was subsequently attacked as a liar who fabricated the presidential affair for money, but four Arkansas state troopers confirmed her story. The troopers acknowledged they had taken hundreds of calls from Flowers for Clinton. They also admitted to driving Clinton to her apartment and that Clinton had tried to arrange state employment for her.

The conservative *American Spectator* magazine published the troopers' story on December 20, 1993. They stated that part of their routine duties was to facilitate and cover up Clinton's extramarital affairs. They claimed Clinton was juggling about "six steady girlfriends whom we saw two or three times a week." They also claimed to run interference with Hillary to prevent Bill from being caught in the act. One trooper, Danny Ferguson, claimed he was offered a federal job as regional director of the Federal Emergency Management Agency (FEMA) or as a U.S. Marshall. Ferguson's supervisor, Raymond L. "Buddy" Young, who headed Clinton's security detail for two years, eventually did become a FEMA regional director. Troopers Roger Perry and Larry Patterson also claimed they received offers of federal jobs in return for their silence.

Another trooper, L.D. Brown, was the subject in a later edition of *American Spectator* wherein he claimed to have solicited more than one hundred women for Bill Clinton while working on the Governor's security staff between 1982 and 1985.

In 1992, a woman named Sally Perdue claimed to have had a three-month affair with Bill beginning in August 1983. In an interview on *The Sally Jesse Raphael Show*, Perdue, a former Miss Arkansas, said she met Clinton in the early seventies when she worked as a reporter for Little Rock's PBS station. Perdue wasn't worried about Clinton's marital status because she saw the fling as a temporary distraction. She claimed Clinton smoked marijuana regularly, saying it "enhanced his sexual pleasure."

For unknown reasons the episode, which was recorded before a studio audience, was never broadcast. In a later interview published in London's *Sunday Telegraph*, Perdue contended she had been offered a high-paying job during the 1992 presidential campaign to keep her mouth shut. L.D. Brown told the *American Spectator* that Clinton had told him about having sex with Perdue.

Bobbie Ann Williams, an African-American woman and former prostitute who worked Little Rock's Hooker's Row, claimed she had been paid to have sex with Bill Clinton on a number of occasions in 1984. According to Bobbie Ann, she received $200 for giving Bill a blow job during their first encounter and later set up an orgy with two other hookers who were paid $400 each. Williams said she and Bill would have regular late-night rendezvous at the Holiday Inn. She also insists Bill Clinton is the father of her son, Danny, who was born in 1985.

In May of 1995, nineteen-year-old Monica Lewinsky took an apartment at the Watergate with her mother, Marsha Lewis, after the two moved to Washington so Monica could work as an unpaid intern for Leon Panetta, President Clinton's chief of staff. Monica had recently graduated from Lewis and Clark College in Portland, Oregon, and started as a White House intern in time for the government shutdown that occurred in late 1995. During the shutdown, Monica and President Clinton saw a lot of each other because many executive employees were not permitted to show up for work. Lewinsky said her affair with Clinton began on November 15, 1995, and lasted, on and off, until 1997. On November 26, 1995, with her internship at an end, Monica was given a full-time paid position at the White House.

Evelyn Lieberman, the deputy chief of staff, noticed the unusual amount of time Lewinsky spent around the Oval Office. Although she denies suspecting an affair, Lieberman arranged for Lewinsky's transfer out of the White House to the Pentagon in April 1996. But Monica wasn't swayed. She continued to show up around the Oval Office, usually under the pretext of visiting Betty Currie, the President's personal secretary.

At her job at the Pentagon, Monica made friends with fellow government worker Linda Tripp, who had also held a position at the White House. Tripp had issues with the way the White House was run when the Clinton administration took over.

The sexual relationship between Monica and Bill seemed pretty much one way—with her performing oral sex on him, and he, well, just enjoying. They also had phone sex. Either growing bored with Lewinsky, or perhaps feeling pressure from Paula Jones's sexual harassment suit, the President tried to end the affair several times, ultimately succeeding.

But Monica still had the President's attention, and she began to pressure him to get her back to a White House position. The more unhappy she became at the Pentagon, the more she whined to Linda Tripp, who, unbeknownst to Lewinsky, had started recording their telephone conversations. The tapes eventually made their way to independent investigator Ken Starr's inquiry.

On December 17, 1997, Lewinsky was subpoenaed to testify in the Paula Jones sexual harassment lawsuit. Washington power broker and Clinton administration friend Vernon Jordan arranged legal counsel for Ms. Lewinsky. On January 7, 1998, she signed a falsified affidavit denying a sexual relationship with the President, but two weeks later, on January 21, the *Washington Post* ran an exposé alleging the Clinton-Lewinsky affair. The President adamantly denied the affair, at one point waving his finger and admonishing the media, "I want you to listen to me. I'm going to say this again: I did not have sexual relations with that woman—Miss Lewinsky." The next day, Hillary defended Bill on *The Today Show*, contending the allegations were false and part of a "vast right-wing conspiracy that had been conspiring against my husband since the day he announced for president."

Ken Starr saw it differently. During his investigation into whether the President perjured himself in the civil deposition, encouraged Lewinsky to lie, and obstructed justice, details about the affair emerged. The most notorious detail involved presidential semen spewing on Monica's blue dress, which she saved un-dry-cleaned as, perhaps, a souvenir. Bill Clinton contended that blow jobs, if you're on the receiving end, don't count, making him an unlikely folk hero among American men.

Monica Lewinsky

Now, like, I'm president. It would be pretty hard for some drug guy to come into the White House and start offering it up, you know? I bet if they did, I hope I would say, "Hey, get lost. We don't want any of that." —George W. Bush talking to students about drug use

PART THREE

Partying

with the

There are blessed intervals when I forget by one means or another that I am President of the United States. —Woodrow Wilson

THE OFFICE OF THE PRESIDENT IS SEEN AS a grand and serious position, but we can't forget that the people who occupy that office are human—and enjoy a good party as much as the rest of us. Through the years, some have even liked parties a lot more than the rest of us. They liked to drink, to smoke, to feast, to dance, to live the high life. Some liked to wear the proverbial lampshade, while others drank to forget painful experiences. Some enjoyed the fancy gatherings of Washington society, while others preferred a rowdier crowd. Let's take a look at some presidents who raised a glass or two or five or ten.

Presidents

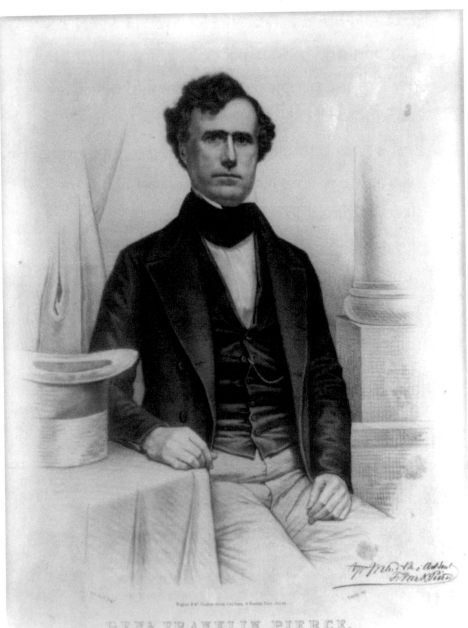

GEN: FRANKLIN PIERCE,
Democratic Candidate for the Presidency.

President Franklin Pierce

1

Drinking to Forget

THE YEAR 1853 BEGAN FULL OF PROMISE for president-elect Franklin Pierce when, just weeks before the first family was scheduled to move to Washington, tragedy struck. The Pierces' eleven-year-old son, Bennie, died in a train wreck in Andover, Massachusetts. He was caught under a train car and crushed to death while Franklin and Jane Pierce watched help-lessly. Jane Pierce was so stricken with grief she was unable to act as first lady for nearly two years. Jane blamed Franklin for the Pierce fam-ily's uprooting from their New Hampshire home and for Bennie's death.

Jane Pierce believed God had a vendetta against the Pierce family, causing the many woes that befell the first family.

Mrs. Pierce believed that their family in general, and President Pierce in particular, were being punished by God. Further evidence of the Lord's apparent wrath came with the sudden unexpected death of Pierce's close friend, New Hampshire Senator Charles G. Atherton, an alleged alcoholic who didn't make it to the inauguration.

The grieving President turned to the bottle to deaden the pain of Bennie's loss and to deal with his wife's bitterness. Soon critics began to claim that President Pierce was a chronic alcoholic incapable of performing his duties to the nation. But, despite his affection for whiskey and much-publicized drinking binges (which included his being slapped with what amounted to a DUI for running over an old woman in the presidential carriage—although it was never proven), Franklin Pierce managed the affairs of the United States until he left office in 1857. During the final days of his presidency, he was asked about his plans for the future. He replied, "There's nothing left . . . but to get drunk."

Last Man Standing

PRESIDENT MARTIN VAN BUREN WAS A LITTLE GUY—BARELY five feet six inches tall and, until late in life, quite thin. But even as a young man he earned a reputation for being able to hold his liquor far better than the big fellas. He could drink all night and not appear to be drunk, a talent that inspired the nickname "Blue Whiskey Van." He apparently drank a lot—and often—throughout his life.

A later president who could have matched him drink for drink was James Buchanan, who was known to consume large amounts of booze without losing his decorum. While those around him slurred and stumbled, Buchanan remained the picture of composure. As a newspaper reporter described him: "All was as cool, as calm and as cautious and watchful as in the beginning. More than one ambitious tyro who sought to follow his . . . example gathered an early fall." ✪

2

Drinking on Duty

ANDREW JOHNSON, BY MOST ACCOUNTS, was a drinker. His affection for potable spirits was first noticed shortly after his arrival in Washington by then-Senator William Stewart of Nevada, who later wrote:

President Andrew Johnson

He came to Washington in January or February, and for some weeks previous to the inauguration of President Lincoln on the fourth of March, 1865, his general condition was a half-drunken stupor. When he entered the Senate chamber to take the oath of office as Vice President, and to call that body to order, he was very drunk. He was assisted to the chair by the Sergeant-at-Arms and two door-keepers, and was unable to stand without assistance. I do not believe he was conscious when he took the oath of office. Immediately after the oath had been administered, he grasped the desk before him with an unsteady hand, and, swaying about so that he threatened to tumble down at any moment, he began an incoherent tirade. . . .

Finally he was removed, not without some force, by the Sergeant-at-Arms to the Vice-President's room, where he was detained until the ceremony was concluded.

Hoping to defend his new vice-president, President Abraham Lincoln told a concerned Treasury Secretary Hugh McCullough, "I have known Andy Johnson for many years; he made a bad slip the other day, but you need not be scared; Andy ain't a drunkard."

Some historians believe Johnson's reputation as a drinker was fueled by political enemies and members of the press who despised his plans for Reconstruction. The official White House spin on Senator Stewart's account was that Andy was "sick with typhoid fever," so he took a few blasts of whiskey to get him through the inauguration, but the liquor went straight to his head.

Perhaps we'll never know for certain, though more than a few contemporaries have written that Johnson frequently enjoyed an eye-opener, whether or not he was feeling poorly.

Demon Weed

ONLY OUR MOST RECENT PRESIDENTS HAVE admitted to smoking marijuana. Bill Clinton swears he never inhaled. George W. Bush seems to have smoked and drank just about anything available during his party-boy younger days. Barack Obama smoked pot in high school—and did his share of cocaine too. Obama says that he continues to struggle with breaking the cigarette habit.

Many of our presidents through the years have enjoyed tobacco in one form or another. Zachary Taylor, who did not touch alcohol, was a chronic chewer of tobacco—and had a reputation of being a talented tobacco-juice spitter. He could bulls-eye a spittoon at ten feet.

John Adams began smoking at the ripe old age of eight. Defying health warnings about the habit, he lived to be ninety.

For many years, Dwight Eisenhower was a four-packs-a-day smoker. In 1949, his doctor warned him that if he didn't cut down he'd ruin his health. The doc prescribed cutting the habit to one pack a day, but counting his daily cigarettes annoyed Ike to no end. So he quit cold turkey and never smoked again.

FDR was another president who loved to smoke cigarettes. While many presidents tried to hide their habit, Roosevelt made it part of his image—tilting a butt in a long holder between his teeth at a jaunty angle.

Martin van Buren, William Henry Harrison, and Gerald Ford preferred a pipe.

Many presidents have enjoyed a good cigar, though none more than Ulysses Grant, who smoked as many as twenty per day. Chester Alan Arthur loved cigars, though would not be seen in public smoking one. The same is true for William McKinley, who felt that the president should set a good example for the country in leading a healthy life.

Warren Harding smoked cigars, as did his successor, Calvin Coolidge. Of course, Harding was usually drinking with the boys when he smoked, while Coolidge enjoyed a quiet, contemplative smoke on the White House porch. Party presidents Kennedy, Johnson, and Clinton all liked a cheroot every now and then, though smoking was banned in the White House during the Clinton administration. Bill sometimes put a cigar in his mouth but he couldn't inhale—or even light it. ✪

ULYSSES S. GRANT,
LIEUTENANT-GENERAL, U.S.A.

President Ulysses S. Grant

180

3

Cocktail Time
for the General

Ulysses S. Grant

"I THEN BEGAN TO ASK THEM IF THEY KNEW
what he drank, what brand of whiskey he used,
telling them most seriously that I wished they
would find out. They conferred with each other
and concluded they could not tell what brand
he used. I urged them to ascertain and let me
know, for if it made fighting generals like Grant
I should like to get some of it for distribution."

—*Abraham Lincoln to a delegation of Congressmen
urging him to fire Grant because he drank too much*

Rumors of the great Union General Ulysses S. Grant's fondness for whiskey on and off the battlefield are firmly implanted in historical lore. But did the man from the small town located where Big Indian Creek meets the Ohio River indeed battle the bottle?

Not long after newlyweds Jesse and Hannah Grant settled in the quiet little town of Point Pleasant in Southwest Ohio, the couple's first son, Ulysses, was born on April 27, 1822. Jesse, the son of an alcoholic, had no tolerance for those not willing to stay sober and work hard. Dedicated to the ideals of earnest labor and proper education, Jesse planned to procure an appointment for his eldest son to the United States Military Academy at West Point. Like many other cadets at the time, this was young Ulysses' first exposure to alcohol.

Early nineteenth century Americans enjoyed their drink, consuming liquor because they believed it was nutritious, stimulated digestion, and relaxed the nerves. Potable spirits were also consumed to accompany food, which was often undercooked, greasy, salty, and sometimes rancid. When Grant graduated from West Point in 1843 and took his place as a second lieutenant in the small, professional army, drinking among the troops was widespread and generally accepted. The young officer took on the habit with his peers. He is known to have indulged frequently while serving in the Mexican War. By the time he returned from the war in 1848, he married and was assigned to an isolated garrison in New York Harbor, where he coped with boredom by hitting the bottle. By 1851, worried about his increasingly heavy drinking, Ulysses joined the Sons of Temperance and became an active participant in the temperance movement.

Transfers and different duties soon proved to be powerful motivators to lure Grant back to drinking, however. By 1853 the young officer found his assignment in northern California so tedious he frequently drank liquor with the boys at a local trading post. One night he apparently drank too many and appeared for duty under the influence. The post commander, Lt. Col. Robert Buchanan, strongly disapproved, instructing Grant to draft a letter of resignation to keep at hand. A short time later, a similar instance of late-night hard drinking compelled Buchanan to give Grant the ultimatum of submitting the resignation or face a Court Martial for being drunk on duty. Captain Grant chose the former.

Although drinking in the military was common and widely accepted in 1854, Grant was incautious about when he indulged. On April 11 of that year, he tendered his resignation to the secretary of war. After fifteen years in the army, Grant returned to civilian life, where history shows he seemed to have little inclination or time to drink.

With the outbreak of the Civil War in 1861, Grant offered his services to the recently appointed commander of the Ohio Militia, Major General James B. McClellan. He received no response, so he made another offer to Brigadier General Nathaniel Lyon, who also did not respond. Evidently, Grant's reputation as a drunk preceded him.

Disappointed, he returned to his family tannery in Galena, Illinois, where he went about mustering volunteers into service. An Illinois congressman noticed Grant's efforts and persuaded the state's governor to appoint Grant as a colonel of the 21st Illinois Infantry Regiment. The 21st had a reputation as a problem regiment, but Grant quickly whipped it into shape, a move that earned him a promotion to Brigadier General by July 1861.

Jealousy ran deep among the ranks of command officers in the Union army, and detractors spread rumors of Grant's boozing, which they knew had led to his resignation years before. Although Grant did begin drinking again prior to the Battle of Shiloh in April 1862, there are no witnesses to validate that he was drunk at the time. Rumors, however, spread quickly that he was drunk while in command. Despite the rumors, Grant forged on.

The well-documented instances of the General's drinking habits came around May 1863 during the Union Army's siege of the

Walking the Line

GRANT ONCE RECEIVED WHAT AMOUNTED TO A speeding ticket for riding his horse too fast on a street in Washington and nearly knocking over a pedestrian. Wags of the time surmised that he was drunk. Either way, the police impounded his horse and issued a twenty-dollar fine. He walked back to the White House. ⭐

Mississippi River port city of Vicksburg. The first happened on May 12, 1863, when a newspaper reporter, Sylvanus Cadwallader, attached himself to Grant's staff to follow the campaign. Cadwallader and Grant's chief of artillery, Colonel William Duff, were sitting inside Duff's tent when the General stepped in. Duff produced a cup and dipped it into a barrel he had stored in the tent. Grant emptied the contents and proceeded to guzzle down two refills. When Grant departed, Cadwallader learned the barrel contained whiskey.

Less than a month later, Cadwallader encountered General Grant aboard the steamboat *Diligence* on a cruise down the Yazoo River. "I was not long in perceiving that Grant had been drinking heavily," Cadwallader remembered, "And that he was still keeping it up. He made several trips to the bar room of the boat in a short time, and became stupid in speech and staggering in gait. This was the first time he had shown symptoms of intoxication in my presence, and I was greatly alarmed by his condition, which was fast becoming worse." According to Cadwallader, General Grant's drinking binge lasted two more days.

When Grant and several of his staff went to review the troops outside of New Orleans, shortly after the victory at Vicksburg, his horse stumbled and fell, injuring Grant. Rumors proliferated among the rank and file that the General was riding under the influence. Other examples, mere gossip or fact unknown, abound.

Amidst the documented accounts, gossip, and rumor that have found their way into history, the question remains: Was Ulysses S. Grant an alcoholic? Author James McPherson says, by today's standards, yes. But, in his book *Battle Cry of Freedom: The Civil War Era*, McPherson contends that Grant's drinking habit may have actually helped in his famous military accomplishments. He writes:

> In the end . . . his predisposition to alcoholism may have made him a better general. His struggle for self-discipline enabled him to understand and discipline others; the humiliation of pre-war failures gave him a quiet humility that was conspicuously absent from so many generals with a reputation to protect; because Grant had nowhere to go but up, he could act with more boldness and decision than commanders who dared not risk failure.

And so it seems that Abraham Lincoln's plan for distribution of cocktails to his military staff may have had more substance than mere presidential sarcasm.

President Chester Alan Arthur

4

The Dude Abides

ONE OF OUR LEAST REMEMBERED presidents, Chester Alan Arthur, was also one of our greatest White House partiers. Taking on the job of Chief Executive after the assassination of James Garfield in 1881, Arthur ushered in a wave of lavish, late-night extravaganzas that featured the best food and booze the Washingtons elite could want.

Arthur was the ideal host for these parties. A portly gent with mutton-chop sideburns, Arthur was a stylish dresser who prided himself on his extensive wardrobe as well as his courtly manners. His nicknames included "Prince Arthur," "Elegant Arthur," "The Gentleman Boss," and "The Dude President." He was a gourmand, who savored rich food and relished fine wines as well as after-dinner liqueurs with a good cigar.

His parties lasted to all hours, and the White House staff didn't expect to see him awake until late morning. Some historians speculate that he led the high life to fill the void of his wife's sudden death from pneumonia at the age of forty-two, less than a year before his election as vice president. Arthur made it known that he would not marry again, though his social charm, elegant dress, and life-of-the-party personality attracted many an interested lady from Washington society.

Others speculate that Arthur knew he was living on borrowed time and was trying to make the most of the situation. He suffered

Ellen, the wife of Chester A. Arthur, died at the age of forty-two.

from a number of ailments, but an incurable kidney condition known then as Bright's Disease meant his days were numbered.

Through the partying lifestyle he ballooned to more than 220 pounds, and he complained often of exhaustion and gastrointestinal disorders. But he managed to be an effective Chief Executive, creating reforms in Civil Service that meant defying the cronies of his rather corrupt past in New York politics. Those who expected his administration to be a free-for-all of corruption turned out to be mistaken. His years in office passed without scandal. As for the evening parties, it's not known if Arthur hooked up with any of the women seeking to make him a married man again—or to at least make him less lonely for an evening. Arthur kept mum on the subject, stating, "I may be President of the United States, but my private life is nobody's damned business."

Hayes E. Days

IF CHET ARTHUR'S WHITE HOUSE WAS PARTY CENTRAL during his administration, his predecessor Rutherford B. Hayes presided over the dullest of years for Washington's fast crowd. After moving into the presidency in 1877, Hayes banned all forms of alcohol from the White House. Though he and his wife, Lucy, were not supporters of the growing temperance movement, they felt the White House should be above moral reproach.

Their parties quickly became known for being most proper—and most boring. The socialites dubbed the first lady "Lemonade Lucy," and the President was seen as dull—even foolish—for adhering to his strict code. One of the best lines about the situation was stated by Secretary of State William Evarts who, when asked about a White House dinner, responded, "Splendid! Water flowed like champagne." ✪

Just One More

GROVER CLEVELAND LIKED TO DRINK BEER, AND HE had the belly to prove it. He was known as "Big Steve" to his friends—he used "Grover" because he thought it had a more serious ring to it—and he could knock back the suds with the best of them. According to presidential lore, one time Cleveland and a friend decided to limit themselves to four beers per day—for the sake of their health and their waistlines. But they quickly concluded that four beers weren't nearly enough to get them through an evening, so when they got together again they decided to "borrow" four-beer rations from the future. After a number of beer-stained evenings, they realized they'd drunk enough beer to use up rations for the rest of the year. So the next time they got together, each brought with him a very large tankard so that "four" beers would be plenty to satisfy them. ✪

5

Prohibition, Poker, Bathtub Gin, and Hangin' with Warren G.

Warren G. Harding

OHIO'S U.S. SENATOR WARREN G. Harding wasn't the most clever politician in Washington, but he recognized the political potential of a noisy group of voters speaking out about the evils of liquor and the saloons where it was served. He also noticed the country was rife enough with wartime patriotism to sway uncommitted voters toward stricter morality. Seizing what he saw as political opportunity, Senator Harding jumped on the Prohibition bandwagon, becoming one of Congress's staunchest proponents of a booze-free society.

Hypocritical as it was, Harding managed to be a leader in passage of the Volstead Act, the popular name for the National Prohibition Act, which was enacted by Congress despite President Woodrow Wilson's veto on October 28, 1919. The same voting public elected Warren G. the country's twenty-ninth president in 1920, making him the first chief executive to take office during Prohibition.

But Warren sure didn't practice what he preached. He was a charter member of the "Ohio Gang" that made up the nucleus of the Harding administration. Warren G. enjoyed good liquor, poker, and fast women. Consequently, the administration charged with keeping America "dry" was the "wettest" to ever occupy the White House.

Harding crony Alice Longworth described the "upstairs/downstairs" atmosphere at the White House, where ordinary guests were kept downstairs and served fruit juices while special guests were ushered upstairs where "trays with bottles containing every imaginable brand of whiskey stood about." The President, Longworth added, "was not a bad man. He was just a slob."

Among his upstairs pals, the President scoffed at the very law he was so instrumental in enacting. He was elected on a promise to return the nation to a state of "normalcy" disrupted by wartime shortages and a global morality wrought by the Wilson administration.

Would You Take a Check?

WARREN HARDING ONCE HAD A BAD NIGHT AT HIS weekly poker game, losing all of the cash in his pocket—and all the White House china. Perhaps he drank too much Prohibition hootch, which was brought every week by Jesse Smith, a corrupt administrator at the Justice Department. ✪

THE GENII OF INTOLERANCE
A DANGEROUS ALLY FOR THE CAUSE OF WOMEN SUFFRAGE

Despite the passage and implementation of the National Prohibition Act, it was tough to find anybody in the country who supported it. President Harding surely didn't. He hosted weekly poker parties that included an open bar supplied by confiscated bootleg hooch.

What the country got was wild and reckless abandon that became known as the "Roaring Twenties." Prohibition became a national joke that was all but impossible to enforce, not that Warren G. had any interest in doing so.

According to some sources, the White House whiskey supply came from Prohibition Bureau raids. Congressmen maintained their own hidden drinking joints and virtually no members took the law seriously.

And the One You Rode in On

WILLIAM HOWARD TAFT WEIGHED OVER THREE HUNDRED pounds during his years in the White House and was advised to get more exercise. Taking the advice, he once sent a telegram to Secretary of War Elihu Root, saying, "Took long horseback ride today; feeling fine." Root responded, "How's the horse?" ✪

6
JFK and Dr. Feelgood

JOHN FITZGERALD KENNEDY BASED HIS 1960 presidential campaign on the idea of a "New Frontier." Originally just a campaign slogan, the phrase developed into a label for the Kennedy administration's domestic and foreign programs. Kennedy told Democratic convention-eers at the 1961 Los Angeles convention:

President John F. Kennedy

Writer Truman Capote was also a "patient" of Dr. Feelgood and enjoyed the same amphetamine-laced elixir as the Kennedys.

We stand at the edge of a New Frontier—the frontier of unfulfilled hopes and dreams, a frontier of unknown opportunities and beliefs in peril. Beyond that frontier are uncharted areas of science and space, unsolved problems of peace and war, unconquered problems of ignorance and prejudice, unanswered questions of poverty and surplus.

He adopted the slogan, "It's time to get this country moving again." But his own movement was fueled by a not-so-natural high. Sometime in the late 1950s, JFK discovered the wonders of speed. Since childhood, he had struggled with poor health and had eventually found relief in Cortisone.

But then he moved on to something "better." He met the legendary "Dr. Feelgood," Max Jacobson, a German immigrant who set up shop in Manhattan in 1936. The doc quickly became famous

as the "physician to the stars" with his "miracle tissue regenera-
tor" that was actually a combination of vitamins, painkillers, human
placenta, and amphetamines. Jacobson's other patients included de-
signer Emilio Pucci and writers Truman Capote and Tennessee Williams. Both Jack and Jacqueline Kennedy became Feelgood patients
during Jack's 1960 presidential campaign.

When JFK was sworn in as the thirty-fifth President of the United States on January 20, 1961, Dr. Feelgood was in the audience
nearby. When the President and first lady made their first state visit
to Paris and Vienna in June of the same year, Jacobson was in tow.
The doctor's magic shots were so indispensable to the Kennedys by
then, they chartered an Air France jet to fly him to Paris. Dr. Feelgood even appeared in family portraits included in Mark Shaw's
John F. Kennedy: A Family Album. Ironically, when Shaw died in
1969 of amphetamine poisoning while under Jacobson's care, the
government investigation that ensued resulted in Dr. Feelgood's
conviction for fraud and forty-eight counts of unprofessional conduct. It's unclear how long JFK enjoyed, or indeed needed, Dr. Feelgood's drug-laced cocktails.

Puritan Prez

THE CHIEF EXECUTIVE LEAST ENAMORED OF WINE, WOMEN,
and song was Millard Fillmore, who managed to survive a term in office
without a single scandal. He was obsessed with leading a healthy life—he
never smoked or drank and was never seen so much as flirting with a woman
at a social gathering. Though largely forgotten and seen by historians as
largely ineffectual, he deserves at least one mention in this book—and this
is it. ✪

After abusing alcohol and pills for many years, Betty Ford conquered her addiction.

7

A Brand New Ford

PRESIDENT GERALD FORD AND HIS WIFE, Betty, had a problem that is all too common in the United States. For more than a decade, including her time as first lady, Betty Ford abused alcohol and drugs—mostly pain killers. Her addiction started as many do, with a drink at cocktail hour. But cocktail hour blew out of control when she began drinking all day long, usually alone. The pills started as a remedy for a pinched nerve, but after prolonged use she became addicted to them.

Betty struggled with her addiction through her family's entire time in the White House. The Ford children were forced to ascertain their mother's condition before bringing friends home for fear of discovery the first lady was a drunk. Given her natural outgoing and unconventional personality, the public did not perceive that there was an issue, and she remained popular with Americans.

cocktail hour **blew** *out of control*

The problem of her addictions compounded when she required treatment for breast cancer. In 1978, the frustrated family intervened and confronted her about the drug and alcohol abuse. She agreed to treatment and was able to conquer her addictions. A silver lining was added to her recovery when, in 1982, she established the Betty Ford Center in Rancho Mirage, California. The center has become world renowned for the treatment of chemical addictions.

Not-So-Cool Cal

CALVIN COOLIDGE WAS ANOTHER NON-PARTYING president, though he didn't have James Polk's work ethic. In fact, he usually worked a four-hour day. He slept at least ten hours a day. He was known mostly for his taciturn personality and for rarely saying more than a few words at a time. He napped every afternoon. When he died, humorist Dorothy Parker asked, "How can they tell?" ✪

Nose to the Grindstone

JAMES KNOX POLK WAS NOT BELOVED AS A PRESIDENT, though he may have been our hardest working Chief Executive. He cut a fine figure at Washington parties and was socially graceful, but he burned the candle on only one end—typically working very long days. His work habits allowed him to achieve nearly all of his goals in the White House, but they also destroyed his health. Three months after he left office, he died of exhaustion at the age of only fifty-three. Perhaps the Party Presidents were right after all. ✪

8

Good Ol' Boys 'n' Beer

Billy Carter

JIMMY CARTER'S "FIRST BROTHER," BILLY, was a colorful character who endeared himself to the American public during the 1976 presidential campaign with his beer-swilling, down-home, good-natured disposition. An apparent expert on beer and beer drinking, Billy told *Playboy* magazine that he preferred Pabst Blue Ribbon because, "I like Robert, the Pabst delivery guy." Billy turned his beer-drinking hobby into cash by endorsing a brew as its namesake. "Billy Beer" was introduced to American beer aficionados in 1977. It was produced by the Falls City Brewing Company of Louisville, Kentucky. Dismal sales figures brought a quick end to the brand, but millions of cans were produced.

Billy personalized every can of Billy Beer with his signature and a few words of beer-drinking wisdom:

> Brewed expressly for and with the personal approval of one of America's all-time great beer drinkers—Billy Carter.

> I had this beer brewed just for me. I think it's the best I've ever tasted. And I've tasted a lot. I think you'll like it, too.

When Billy Beer ceased production, advertisements appeared in newspapers offering Billy Beer cans to collectors for hundreds or even thousands of dollars each. But because they were produced in mass quantities, the cans are available today for pennies on sites like eBay.

Billy's antics were a cause of some embarrassment for his straight-laced brother and for those in the Carter administration. Financial problems and public displays—which included urinating on an airport runway—kept Billy in the news, especially for his suspicious dealings with the Libyan government, from which Billy took a $220,000 loan. The scandal, called "Billygate" by the press, didn't amount to much, but it didn't help Jimmy's already flagging image.

Billy sought treatment for alcoholism in 1979 but remained a boisterous, unruly character. After what President Jimmy Carter described as a "battle with alcoholism and recovery," Billy Carter died of pancreatic cancer in 1988 at the age of fifty-one.

Jimmy Carter and his colorful younger brother, Billy.

JIMMY CARTER HAS THE UNIQUE DISTINCTION OF BEING the only U.S. President to officially report a UFO sighting. It was October of 1969 when Mr. Carter, an up-and-coming young politician, was scheduled to speak to a monthly meeting of the local Lion's Club in the small Georgia town of Leary. Outside of the hall, Carter saw a "remarkable sight" in the night sky that inspired him to dictate details of the occasion into his portable tape recorder.

It wasn't until four years later, when Carter was Georgia's governor, that he filled out a form officially documenting his sighting. Governor Carter described the UFO as a bright "bluish" object nearly the size of the distant moon. He estimated that it was no farther than a thousand yards away from where he stood. He said it moved away and then closer, finally disappearing and turning reddish in color as it did.

When it comes to UFOs, there are skeptics and there are believers. Jimmy Carter clarified his opinion a couple years after that night in Leary when he said, "I don't laugh at people anymore when they say they've seen UFOs. I've seen one myself." ✪

President George H. W. Bush

9

Skeletons in the Nominee's Closet

EVERYBODY IN WASHINGTON SEEMED surprised when the Senate voted on March 9, 1989, to reject President George H.W. Bush's nomination of former-Senator John Tower as Secretary of Defense. Tower, a prominent Texan, knew his way around Washington, having served twenty-four years in the Senate before serving in a number of capacities in the Reagan administration, including head of the Iran-contra investigation. It was the first rejection of a presidential cabinet nominee in more than thirty years.

But, perhaps John Tower's fifty-three to forty-seven vote of no confidence had something to do with his D.C. old-timer's reputation. Three issues came to light. First, Tower was renowned as a womanizer. National headlines described him dancing naked with a Russian ballerina atop a piano. The son of a Methodist minister, he also allegedly fondled a female member of the military in front of thousands of people.

The second issue was Tower's drinking. The FBI prepared a report, at the Senate's request, that stated Tower displayed "a clear pattern of excessive drinking and alcohol abuse" during the 1970s. Problems with alcohol disqualified any person from certain senior positions in the Defense Department, much less Secretary.

Finally, certain Senators saw Tower's previous employment as a lobbyist and consultant for the defense industry as a conflict of interest in that Tower would have the power to award huge government contracts to his former employers.

The new President's reputation wasn't tarnished by association with Tower other than that it demonstrated misguided cronyism— like Bush, Tower was a Texas Republican, and so his previous transgressions were overlooked because he was part of the good-old-boy network.

And so, John Tower, a Wild and Crazy Guy of the '70s, left his government career there.

He may have looked like Yoda, but John Tower found his Force in women, wine, and song . . . not necessarily in that order.

Guess Who's Coming to Dinner

TEDDY ROOSEVELT HADN'T BEEN IN THE WHITE House a month in 1901 when, as new presidents often do, he invited a prominent American to dinner. It was a brand new century for America, so Roosevelt didn't anticipate controversy after the two men sat down in the presidential dining room with the first lady, Edith, and a family friend. But controversy is exactly what Roosevelt got.

President Roosevelt's guest was Booker T. Washington, the head of Tuskegee University and the first African-American to be invited to dine at the White House. Public reaction, especially in the South, was explosive. Southern newspapers portrayed the visit as scandalous. "White men of the South, how do you like it?" complained the front page of the *New Orleans Times Democrat*, followed by, "White women of the South, how do YOU like it?" The headlines of other papers were every bit as bigoted. "A Damnable Outrage," read the *Memphis Scimitar*. The *Richmond Dispatch* declared, "Roosevelt Dines a Darkey."

Politicians across the South joined the press in condemning Roosevelt. "No self-respecting Southern man can ally himself with the President after what has occurred," the governor of Georgia complained. "Social equality with the Negro means decadence and damnation!" said South Carolina Lieutenant Governor James Tillman. Hate mail, and even death threats, rained into the White House.

"No one could possibly be as astonished as I was," Roosevelt wrote to a friend. To his critics he said, "I shall have him to dine just as often as I please." Nonetheless, while Booker T. Washington made subsequent visits to Roosevelt at the White House, there are no reports the two ever sat down to dinner together again. ✪

President William Jefferson Clinton

10

Never Inhale

LIKE A LOT OF OTHER ISSUES, BILL CLINTON
dodged questions about drug use for years.
When he ran for governor of Arkansas in 1986,
he was asked if he had ever used drugs. He said
no. By 1989, the answer changed to he had
never used drugs as an adult in Arkansas. The
question was asked again during the 1990 gubernatorial campaign, and this time he said he
"had never violated the drug laws of the state."
By 1991, an *Arkansas Gazette* reporter refined
the question, asking if he had ever smoked marijuana in college. Clinton said "no." Later that
year, in a speech to the National Press Club,

Clinton stated that he had never violated any state or federal drug laws.

When the press persisted in pinning him down, Clinton finally relented during a 1992 primary debate, saying, "When I was in England I experimented with marijuana a time or two, and I didn't like it. I didn't inhale it, and never tried it again." Interestingly, two of Bill's former girlfriends disputed this claim. Gennifer Flowers and Sally Perdue both allege Clinton smoked marijuana in their presence.

Most critics didn't care as much about Bill's smoking marijuana jay as they were about the lengths he had gone to cover it up. But he finally did ease up in a later MTV interview, where he told a group of kids that if he had it all to do over again—he'd go ahead and inhale.

Kicking the Habit

IF BILL CLINTON WAS FIBBING IN HIS CLAIM THAT HE had smoked marijuana but hadn't inhaled, he would have been telling the truth if asked about smoking cigars in the White House. First Lady Hillary Clinton banned smoking in the presidential home, and her rule included her husband, who enjoyed a good cigar. Bill stuck to the rule, though he was secretly photographed at least twice in the Oval Office with a cigar in his mouth—though the cheroot remained unlit. Bill's love of cigars achieved national notoriety during the Monica Lewinsky scandal, when he allegedly used a cigar tube to "not have sex" with his intern. ✪

11

D. Dubya I.

GEORGE W. BUSH FINALLY ADMITTED THAT he was convicted of driving drunk. On September 4, 1976, a Maine state trooper saw Bush's car swerve onto the shoulder, then back onto the road. Bush failed a field sobriety test and blew a .10 blood alcohol on the intoxylizer. He pled guilty to the charge, received a fine, and had his driver's license suspended. His spokesman said he had "several beers" at a local bar before the arrest. W. was thirty years old at the time. He later said he stopped drinking when he turned forty because the habit had become a problem.

When the arrest came up during the presidential campaign of 2000, George seemed more annoyed than repentant or remorseful. He even went on the offensive, asking reporters, "Why [was this reported] now, four days before the election? I've got my suspicions." In fact, it was a fellow DWI defendant in court the same day who revealed Bush' arrest. Here's what W. said in his press conference:

Bush: I told the guy I had been drinking and what do I need to do? And he said, "Here's the fine." I paid the fine and did my duty. . . .

Reporter: Governor, was there any legal proceeding of any kind? Or did you just—

Bush: No. I pled—you know, I said I was wrong and I—

Reporter: In court?

Bush: No, there was no court. I went to the police station. I said, "I'm wrong."

Junior was quite the rascal

W. also got a court hearing in 1978 to get his driving suspension lifted early. He had not completed the required driver rehabilitation course. He told the hearing officer that he drank only once a month, and just had "an occasional beer." The officer granted his request and reinstated W.'s operator's license. Bush continued drinking for eight years after. He later admitted publicly that he drank too much and had a drinking problem during that time.

Apparently, the bottle didn't only cause W. problems behind the wheel. In another incident, he started screaming profanities at a *Wall Street Journal* reporter, who predicted that George H.W. Bush would not be the 1988 Republican presidential nominee. The reporter obviously was wrong, but a drunken Bush Jr. walked up to him at a restaurant and yelled, "You fucking son of a bitch. I won't forget what you said and you're going to pay a price for it."

In his younger and more vulnerable years, W. was distinguished by his hearty appetite for partying. In a *Newsweek* profile, writer Evan Thomas describes the Bush college years by saying "[W.] seems to have majored in beer drinking at the Deke House." After W. formed his first company, which failed, Thomas writes, "By his own account, Bush spent a lot of time in bars, trying to sort out who he was. He had a kind of ragged nervous energy in that period, and he could be a bully."

The Bush family spin is that the governor quit drinking cold turkey on his fortieth birthday, straightened out by the love of a good woman—his wife, Laura. They even pulled out dear old Mom, the lovable Barbara Bush, with anecdotes about how little George Junior was quite a rascal but now was a sweet angel.

Despite his Mother's endorsement, W. wanted to be sure of exactly everything that was in the closet, and so he hired a private investigator to dig into his own past. According to an unnamed insider quoted on MSNBC, Bush "wasn't terribly thrilled" about what the PI found. At least, "no handcuffs or dwarf orgies, but he was a handsome, rich playboy and lived that life," the insider said.

Some say W.'s wild, wild life included cocaine and marijuana use. According to author J.H. Hatfield in *Fortunate Son: George W. Bush and the Making of an American President*, three independent sources close to the Bush family claim that George W. Bush was arrested in 1972 for cocaine possession and taken to the Harris County Jail, but avoided jail or formal charges through an informal diversion plan involving community service with Project P.U.L.L., an inner-city Houston program for troubled youths at the Martin Luther King Jr. Community Center in Houston's dirt-poor Third Ward. That year certainly is out of character with the rest of Bush Jr.'s life. Before and after 1972, he was a hard-drinking playboy. As soon as the year was over, it was party-on business as usual. He's done no charity work since.

President George W. Bush

Misunderestimating George W.

WITH ALL DUE RESPECT TO WARREN G. HARDING, President George W. Bush provided America with the most amusing, albeit sometimes confusing, public statements in presidential history. They were quoted by foe and friend alike and even made into desk calendars. Here are a few samples of W. on the record:

"One of the interesting initiatives we've taken in Washington, D.C., is we've got these vampire-busting devices. A vampire is a—a cell deal you can plug in the wall to charge your cell phone." — *Denver, CO. Aug. 14, 2001*

"Well, it's an unimaginable honor to be the president during the Fourth of July of this country. It means what these words say, for starters. The great inalienable rights of our country. We're blessed with such values in America. And I—it's—I'm a proud man to be the nation based upon such wonderful values." —*Visiting the Jefferson Memorial, Washington, D.C., July 2, 2001*

"We spent a lot of time talking about Africa, as we should. Africa is a nation that suffers from incredible disease." —*After meeting with the leaders of the European Union, Gothenburg, Sweden, June 14, 2001*

"I've coined new words, like, misunderstanding and Hispanically." —*Radio-Television Correspondents Association dinner, Washington, D.C., March 29, 2001*

"I am mindful not only of preserving executive powers for myself, but for predecessors as well." —*Washington, D.C., Jan. 29, 2001*

"Then I went for a run with the other dog and just walked. And I started thinking about a lot of things. I was able to—I can't remember what it was. Oh, the inaugural speech, started thinking through that." —*Pre-inaugural interview with U.S. News & World Report, Jan. 22, 2001 issue*

"Redefining the role of the United States from enablers to keep the peace to enablers to keep the peace from peacekeepers is going to be an assignment." —*Interview with the New York Times, Jan. 14, 2001*

"The California crunch really is the result of not enough power-generating plants and then not enough power to power the power of generating plants." —*Interview with the New York Times, Jan. 14, 2001*

"They misunderestimated me." —*Bentonville, Ark., Nov. 6, 2000*

"I know how hard it is for you to put food on your family." —*Greater Nashua, N.H., Chamber of Commerce, Jan. 27, 2000*

"I know the human being and fish can coexist peacefully." —*Saginaw, Mich., Sept. 29, 2000*

"The great thing about America is everybody should vote." —*Austin, Texas, Dec. 8, 2000*

"It's clearly a budget. It's got a lot of numbers in it." —*Reuters, May 5, 2000*

"Rarely is the question asked: Is our children learning?" —*Florence, S.C., Jan. 11, 2000*

"I understand small business growth. I was one." —*New York Daily News, Feb. 19, 2000*

"The most important job is not to be governor, or first lady in my case." —*Pella, Iowa, as quoted by the San Antonio Express-News, Jan. 30, 2000*

"It's important for us to explain to our nation that life is important. It's not only life of babies, but it's life of children living in, you know, the dark dungeons of the Internet." —*Arlington Heights, Ill., Oct. 24, 2000*

"I think if you know what you believe, it makes it a lot easier to answer questions. I can't answer your question." —*Reynoldsburg, Ohio, Oct. 4, 2000*

"Natural gas is hemispheric. I like to call it hemispheric in nature because it is a product that we can find in our neighborhoods." —*Austin, Texas, Dec. 20, 2000*

"The senator [McCain] has got to understand if he's going to have it he can't have it both ways. He can't take the high horse and then claim the low road." —*To reporters in Florence, S.C., Feb. 17, 2000*

"We ought to make the pie higher." —*South Carolina Republican Debate, Feb. 15, 2000*

"They want the federal government controlling Social Security like it's some kind of federal program." —*Debate in St. Charles, Mo., Nov. 2, 2000*

"It's your money. You paid for it." —*Lacrosse, Wis., Oct. 18, 2000*

"It's not the governor's role to decide who goes to heaven. I believe that God decides who goes to heaven, not George W. Bush." —*George W. Bush, in the Houston Chronicle*

"There ought to be limits to freedom. We're aware of this [web] site, and this guy is just a garbage man, that's all he is." —*Discussing a satirical Web site*

"I'm a uniter not a divider. That means when it comes time to sew up your chest cavity, we use stitches as opposed to opening it up." —*on David Letterman, March 2, 2000.*

"I didn't—I swear I didn't—get into politics to feather my nest or feather my friends' nests." —*as quoted in the Houston Chronicle.*

PART FOUR

Presidential

People in the media say they must look at the president with a microscope. Now, I don't mind a microscope, but boy, when they use a proctoscope, that's going too far. – Richard Nixon

If you can't convince them, confuse them. – Harry Truman

If I had two faces would I be wearing this one? – Abraham Lincoln's response to a heckler calling him "two-faced"

Peccadilloes

I'm not going to have some reporters pawing through our papers. We are the president. – First Lady Hillary Clinton commenting on the release of subpoenaed documents

1
Most Votes = Runner-Up?

THE FIRST ELECTION OF A UNITED STATES president who didn't receive the highest number of votes occurred in 1824. In a four-way race, none of the candidates managed to get the necessary one hundred and thirty-one Electoral College votes to take office, causing the decision to go to the House of Representatives, where some said the presidency was awarded based on a "corrupt bargain."

Tennessean Andrew Jackson managed to garner 41 percent of the popular vote but only ninety-nine electoral votes. John Quincy Adams was second with 31 percent of the popular vote and eighty-four electoral votes. Rounding out the field were Henry Clay of Kentucky with 13 percent of the popular vote and thirty-seven electoral votes and Georgian William Crawford with 11 percent popular and forty-one electoral.

The Constitution provides the solution by sending the vote to the House of Representatives, where each state casts one vote for one of the top three finishers in electoral ballots (meaning that Clay was out).

With the election to be decided "in-house," both Jackson and Adams scrambled for support. Political wheels started to spin. Adams figured that if he won in the House, certain politicians would play hell, even to the point of talk of a civil war. In January of 1825,

President John Quincy Adams

the Kentucky delegation told Adams they were willing to throw their vote his way. The recently disqualified Henry Clay decided to cut his losses by backing Adams—in hopes of nabbing a high government office for himself. (Say hello to Henry Clay, future Secretary of State.)

Ironically, Adams almost dreaded winning under such circumstances, saying: "To me both alternatives are distressing in prospect. The most formidable is that of success. All the danger is on the pinnacle. The humiliation of failure will be so much more compensated by the safety in which it will leave me, that I ought to regard it as a consummation devoutly to be wished, and hope to find consolation in it." He was a man stuck in the middle. Naturally, Henry Clay and his supporters expected to be "taken care of" for their support. But if he delivered as president, Jackson and Crawford were already screaming corruption for the deal.

Jackson and Crawford considered collaborating on a deal between themselves, but they couldn't agree on who got the big prize. When the House voted on February 9, Adams had support from thirteen state delegations to Jackson's seven and Crawford's four. Adams already carried the six New England states and New York, and Clay delivered Kentucky, Missouri, and Ohio. John Q. managed to steal Louisiana, Illinois, and Maryland from a frustrated Andrew Jackson. Adams became the sixth President of the United States.

Jackson and his team immediately cried foul. They claimed a corrupt bargain was struck between former rivals Adams and Clay. Jacksonians launched a campaign to convince voters that a dirty, back-door deal had been made between the new president and Henry Clay and that Adams' election was not the will of the people but the result of corrupt politics.

Clay and Adams both vehemently denied allegations of a quid pro quo. When an anonymous letter accusing the President and Clay of corruption appeared in a Philadelphia newspaper, Clay challenged its author to a duel. An investigation later revealed that the

The Company Dime

DURING THE REVOLUTIONARY WAR, GENERAL GEORGE
Washington agreed to forgo a salary as long as his expenses were reimbursed, sort of like an early American expense account. Or should that be early American padded expense account?

George's expense account included charges for his wife, Martha's, travel and lodging, other's visits to outposts in the field, charges incurred in keeping his slaves, and the keep for his staff like his personal secretary and aide-de-camp. Washington's claimed expenses? They amounted to $449,261, including 6 percent interest on the personal funds he loaned the military—almost ten times the $49,000 salary he would have received. ✪

letter writer was Representative George Kremer of Pennsylvania, who claimed he could substantiate the allegations. Kremer, however, failed to substantiate anything during the investigation.

In the end, no proof was ever found of a corrupt bargain between John Q. Adams and Henry Clay. That didn't stop Andrew Jackson from holding onto the issue. In the next presidential campaign in 1827, Jackson claimed Representative James Buchanan of Pennsylvania had approached him during the previous election to make a similar deal on Clay's behalf. Buchanan, of course, denied the allegation, claiming his call on General Jackson was simply a friendly visit.

Substantiated or not, the corruption scandal crippled John Q. Adams' administration from the start. He lost the next presidential election to his nemesis, Andrew Jackson.

The Trail of Tears

DURING THE EARLY 1830S, THE U.S. GOVERNMENT struggled with the delicate issue of relocating Indian tribes off of "state-owned" property. The Supreme Court was clear in two decisions (*Cherokee Nation v. Georgia*, 1831; *Worchester v. Georgia*, 1832) that identified the federal government, not the states, as having ultimate jurisdiction over American Indian tribes. President Andrew Jackson didn't like the Court's decision because he wanted to avoid a states' rights showdown. The Supreme Court ruling that Georgia had no authority to pass laws affecting Indian lands posed a difficult question about whether Jackson would enforce the verdict.

President Jackson feared tampering with states' rights, but he also feared the ramifications of ignoring the Supreme Court by nullifying Georgia's claim of jurisdiction. Jackson favored the Indians' removal as a method of preserving peace. He pressured the Cherokee nation to move and did nothing to help them retain their land from the unconstitutional advances by the state of Georgia.

The Cherokees themselves were divided on the issue. Those who wanted to stay were often threatened, and their leader, John Ross, went to jail for violating Georgia statutes. Under the Treaty of New Echota, the Cherokees agreed to move west. Terms of the treaty gave the Indians until 1838 to vacate, but white settlers began to push the issue in 1836. Forced out, the Cherokees began a ride on the "Trail of Tears," so-called because more than four thousand of the original sixteen thousand who began the journey died.

Jackson critics accused him of "genocide" because of his refusal to intercede and enforce the Supreme Court decisions or the treaty terms. Supporters claimed Jackson feared for the Indians' safety if they stayed in the East much longer. Whatever his motives, Jackson's inaction and the Trail of Tears catastrophe is one of America's lasting disgraces. ✪

2

Doesn't Play Well with Congress

TENTH PRESIDENT JOHN TYLER HAD A FIERY relationship with a Whig Congress. He wasn't afraid to veto any legislation the Whigs sent his way. When the fourth veto on an economic measure bounced back to the House, Congress didn't bother to put the President's veto message on the record. Instead, they appointed a select committee, including former president John Quincy Adams of Massachusetts and Tyler political enemy John Minor Botts of Virginia, to make a report on President Tyler's veto.

The final report blasted Tyler, claiming the President upset the constitutional balance requiring his office to be "dependent upon and responsible to" Congress. The report continued that Tyler's repeated vetoes disregarded "the whole action of the Legislative authority of the Union." The report cited an example of the President's duplicity by claiming he lied to a certain congressman when he told the congressman he would sign the very bill he'd just vetoed. The report concluded that President Tyler's offense was worthy of impeachment, but impeachment articles were not recommended because the committee felt they could not get such a drastic measure passed through the House. Surprisingly, the House voted by a margin of one hundred to eighty, to adopt the report of the committee, including statements that President Tyler committed impeachable offenses.

guilty of shameless duplicity, equivocation, and falsehood,

On August 30, 1842, Tyler formally protested the committee's report and its adoption by Congress. His protest accused the committee of going out of its way to sensationalize its slanted view of his decisions. Tyler demanded the House bring charges of impeachment so that he could defend himself in a Senate trial. The President insisted that if the charges were true, although he maintained they were not, then he deserved impeachment and removal from office:

> I am charged with offenses against the country so grave and heinous as to deserve public disgrace and disenfranchisement. I am charged with violating pledges which I never gave, with usurping powers not conferred by law, and above all, with using powers conferred upon the

President by the Constitution from corrupt motives and for unwarrantable ends.

The House declined Tyler's protest—nor was it placed on the official record. Instead, the lawmakers criticized the President for challenging the House's privilege to make such a report. Representative John Minor Botts, however, was happy to grant Tyler's request. In January of 1843, he presented nine formal articles of impeachment against the President to the House of Representatives. Six of the charges involved accusations of abuse of power. In reality, the articles involved constitutional duties of the Chief Executive, such as political appointments and removals and veto rights. The other three allegations, however, were legitimate considering Tyler's actions, Botts wrote:

> I charge him with gross official misconduct, in having been guilty of shameless duplicity, equivocation, and falsehood, with his late Cabinet and Congress . . . by which he has brought such dishonor on himself as to disqualify him from administering the Government with advantage, honor, or virtue, and for which alone he would deserve to be removed from office. I charge him with an illegal and unconstitutional exercise of power, in instituting a commission to investigate past transactions under a former administration of the custom house of New York, under the pretense of seeing the laws faithfully executed . . . with having directed or sanctioned the appropriation of large sums of the public revenue to the compensation of officers of his own creation, without the authority of law; which, if sanctioned, would place the entire revenues of the country at his disposal.
>
> I charge him with the high misdemeanor of having withheld from the Representatives of the people infor-

mation called for, and declared to be necessary to the investigation of stupendous frauds and abuses alleged to have been committed by him against the Government itself, whereby he becomes accessory to those frauds.

The House voted one hundred and twenty-seven to eighty-three against appointing a commission to investigate the charges. Once again, the majority didn't believe there were enough votes to force the issue. Because no formal charges were issued, Tyler wasn't required to respond. But he did. He argued that there were occasions the Chief Executive was obligated to assume executive privilege to deny requests for information he considered detrimental to his constitutional obligation to enforce laws. He stated executive privilege was acknowledged by Congress as a legitimate and necessary power derived from the constitutional duties of the presidency. Tyler de-

Many of them gave him the nickname "His Accidency."

nied all information under chief executive control "must necessarily be subject to the call of the House of Representatives merely because they related to a subject of the deliberations of the House." He concluded with, "Certain communications [are] privileged. The general authority to compel testimony must give way in certain cases to the paramount rights of individuals or of the Government."

Tyler's ability to make peace with Congress—and with his own cabinet, for that matter, stemmed from his role as the first vice president to assume the role of president upon the death of the elected chief executive. President William Henry Harrison died within weeks of his tenure, and Vice President Tyler took command. But

The Treasonous President

THE ONLY AMERICAN PRESIDENT TO COMMIT A PUBLIC ACT of treason against his government is John Tyler. In 1860, as Southern states seceded from the Union one after the other, Tyler was fifteen years removed from the U.S. presidency. A life-long advocate of states' rights, he was also a longtime slave owner but publicly called for a compromise between North and South. He chaired a Peace Convention in Washington in February of 1861, avowing "to preserve the Government and to renew and invigorate the Constitution."

At the same time, Tyler engaged in secret correspondence with Confederate president Jefferson Davis. When the Peace Convention failed, Tyler quickly revealed his true allegiance. He encouraged legislators in his native Virginia to join the other Southern states in rebellion. When Virginia did secede from the Union, Tyler became its first representative to the Confederate Congress. He died shortly afterward, a rebel government official at war with the country he had once served as chief executive. ✪

John Tyler

Nothing Free About the Press

WHEN DEMOCRAT JAMES K. POLK BECAME PRESIDENT in 1845, he sought a way to replace *Washington Globe* editor Francis Blair with someone more supportive of the Polk administration. The only problem seemed to be that Polk's choice, Thomas Ritchie, an editor from Virginia, didn't have the money needed to purchase Blair's share of the *Globe*. No problem for President Polk, who immediately ordered half of the $35,000 cost of the paper to be advanced by the Treasurer of the United States against future printing contracts to be awarded to the *Globe*.

The other half of the $35K was drawn from government deposits from a Pennsylvania bank owned by Democratic Senator Simon Cameron. It wasn't until 1847 that Polk's Treasury Secretary, Robert J. Walker, recalled the loan. By that time, the *Globe* not only proved to be a valuable political asset to President Polk, it had become hugely profitable from many lucrative government printing contracts. ✪

many in the federal government felt he should be called the "acting president." Many of them gave him the nickname "His Accidency."

Tyler, however, took the full powers of the office and even defied Whig party leaders, such as the powerful Henry Clay, who had planned on having a lot of influence over Harrison. In the end, Tyler served out the term, making more enemies than any president up to that time. Being president has been called the loneliest job in the world, and for John Tyler that characterization was very true.

3

No Body for
Habeas Corpus

Abraham Lincoln

DURING THE CIVIL WAR, PRESIDENT
Abraham Lincoln feared "the enemy in the
rear." He believed the Confederacy maintained
"a most efficient corps of spies, informers, sup-
pliers, and aiders and abettors" in the northern
states who would use concepts like "Liberty of
speech, Liberty of the press, and Habeas Corpus" to aid the South by disrupting Union war efforts. It was an unprecedented war, and Lincoln
reacted to his fear by taking the unprecedented
actions of suspending Habeas Corpus and au-
thorizing Union army commanders to declare

martial law in certain areas of the Union, allowing them to bring northern civilians to trial in military courts. The President reasoned the restrictions on civil liberties were necessary if "the laws of Union—and freedom itself—were to survive the war."

The State, War, and Navy Departments were bestowed with responsibility for dealing with "disloyal activities." Secretary of State William Seward led the way by censoring telegraph communications and the mail and assigning government agents, U.S. marshals, city police officers, and private informers to surveillance and arrest of "suspicious" persons.

Lincoln noticed Seward's sometimes heavy-handed method of dealing with "suspects" and didn't like it. In May 1861, Lincoln issued a memorandum directing, "unless the necessity for these arbitrary arrests is manifest, and urgent, I prefer they should cease."

By 1862, Lincoln charged Secretary Edwin Stanton's War Department with Union internal security. Stanton enlisted a corps of civilians as "Provost Marshals" who were charged with policing and jailing those suspected of disloyalty to the Union. Often, the marshals abused their arrest powers, acting like common thugs in the eyes of many—particularly critics of Lincoln. Stanton also authorized army officers to arrest any person who spoke out against the draft or who discouraged volunteers for Union service. In all, thirteen thousand people, mostly northern antiwar Democrats (known as "Copperheads"), were arrested and imprisoned merely on suspicion of disloyalty to the Union.

Public outcry about arbitrary arrests and abuse of power grew loud enough to force the President and Secretary Stanton to react. Both tried to reign in overzealous marshals, and both released prisoners under arrest with insufficient cause, especially political prisoners. Union General Ambrose Burnside had gone so far as to suspend publication of the *Chicago Times* for its criticism of President Lincoln and the war. Lincoln promptly revoked the order.

Buchanan's Blunder

RISING CONFLICT OVER FEDERAL JURISDICTION
disputes in the Utah Territory between the government and the
Mormon Church worried President James Buchanan in 1857.
At its peak, Buchanan decided to dispatch a new governor, and
2,500 federal troops, out west to restore order.

When Mormon leader Brigham Young got word of the action,
he prepared for a fight. Young declared martial law, called up the
Mormon militia, and collected arms. Three years before the Civil
War, the United States was threatened with . . . a civil war.

Buchanan's troops had a rotten time reaching Utah. A slow
start put the army smack in the middle of fierce winter weather.
The Mormons raided supply wagons, forcing the troops to survive the winter on starvation rations. Criticism mounted in Washington about the President's handling of the situation. The press
nicknamed the failing effort "Buchanan's Blunder." It was a huge
political embarrassment for the administration.

The government and the Mormons eventually negotiated a
compromise, and the Army entered Salt Lake City peacefully. The
new governor took charge without incident. But, politically, the
damage to Buchanan's reputation was done.

"Buchanan's Blunder" crippled the President's ability to effectively deal with the looming crisis simmering in the South. When
Southern states began to secede from the Union, Buchanan round-
ly refused to send federal troops—perhaps because of the burn his
reputation suffered for the Utah fiasco. As a result, the Southern
rebellion remained unchecked until Abraham Lincoln's election.
One way or the other, the Civil War ultimately cost more than one
million American lives. ✪

THE COPPERHEAD PARTY.——IN FAVOR OF *A VIGOROUS PROSECUTION OF PEACE!*

During the Civil War, "Honest Abe" feared that the Constitution he had taken a solemn oath to protect would be used against the Union. He held the Confederate sympathizing "Copperheads" at bay by suspending every American's Constitutional rights and using the muscle of the Union Army to enforce his dictates.

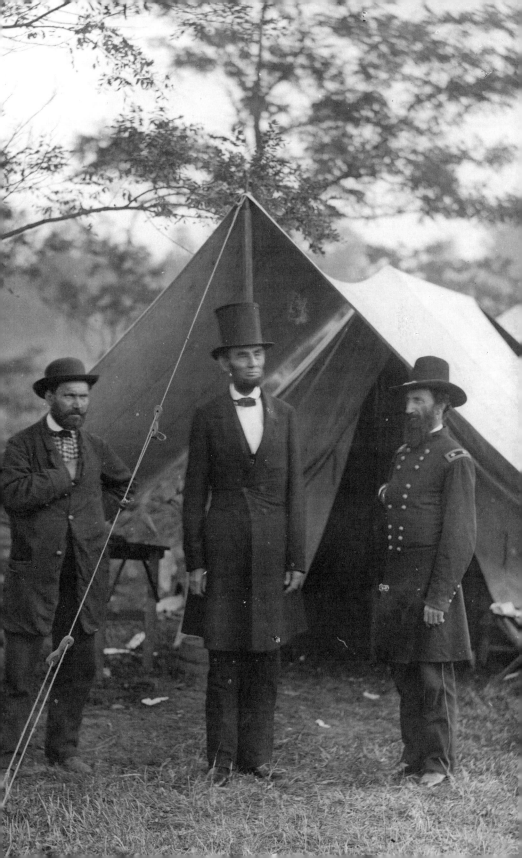

One of the most infamous military arrests of the era was of Ohio Copperhead, and former U.S. Representative from Ohio, Clement L. Vallandigham. In 1863, General Burnside issued General Order Number 38, which warned that the "habit of declaring sympathies for the enemy" would not be tolerated in the Military District of Ohio. Vallandigham disregarded the warning, delivering a major speech to Ohioans in which he said the war had nothing to do with saving the Union but was being fought only to free slaves. To war supporters he warned, "Defeat, debt, taxation, and sepulchers— these are your trophies."

He denounced "King Lincoln," calling for the President's removal from office. On May 5, 1863, Vallandigham was arrested for violation of General Order No. 38. His arrest enraged his supporters, who burned the offices of the *Dayton Journal*, a Republican newspaper.

"Must I shoot a simple-minded soldier boy who deserts, while I must not

Days after his arrest, Vallandigham was tried by a military tribunal, denied a writ of Habeas Corpus, and convicted of "uttering disloyal sentiments and attempting to hinder the prosecution of the war." He was sentenced to two years imprisonment in a military prison. A Federal circuit judge upheld Vallandigham's arrest and military trial as a valid exercise of the President's war powers. President Lincoln wrote to several Ohio politicians offering to release Vallandigham if they agreed to support certain policies of his administration. Lincoln, of course, didn't want Vallandigham considered a martyr to the Copperhead cause, writing, "Must I shoot a simple-minded soldier boy who deserts, while I must not touch a hair of a wily agitator who induces him to desert?"

Lincoln ordered Vallandigham banished through enemy lines to the Confederacy. He was taken under guard to Tennessee. After being deported to the South, Vallandigham hopped a blockade-runner to Bermuda and then went to Canada, where he declared his candidacy for Governor of Ohio. Outraged at his treatment by Lincoln, Ohio Democrats nominated Vallandigham as their candidate in absentia by a vote of 411 to eleven at their June 11, 1863, convention. He managed a campaign from a hotel room in Windsor, Ontario. His platform included Ohio's secession from the Union if President Lincoln refused to immediately reconcile with the Confederate states. Vallandigham lost the gubernatorial election by a landslide to pro-Union War Democrat John Brough. Eventually, Vallandigham returned to Ohio and wasn't shy about appearing in public. He attended the 1864 Democratic National Convention in Chicago, where he delivered the "peace plank" declaring the war a failure and demanding an immediate end of hostilities.

touch a hair of a wily

agitator who induces him to desert?"

Vallandigham returned to Ohio permanently after the war and lost elections for the Senate and House of Representatives on an anti-Reconstruction platform. Finally tired of politics, Vallandigham resumed his law practice. He died in 1871 at the age of fifty. He accidentally shot himself during a murder trial while trying to prove his client innocent. He didn't know the gun was loaded.

President Andrew Johnson

4

A Peach of an Impeachment

Andrew Johnson

IN 1865, IN THE AFTERMATH OF ABRAHAM Lincoln's assassination, Andrew Johnson inherited the presidency and, with it, the problem of reconstructing the Union. Johnson was a stubborn man, known for profane outbursts and rigid stubbornness to the point of appearing to prefer conflict over compromise. Thus, from the beginning of his presidency, Johnson seemed determined to clash with the largely Republican Congress about reconstruction of the recently defeated South.

Johnson possessed a strong bias toward states' rights. He believed the southern states should be re-admitted to the Union as soon as they demonstrated loyalty. He felt there should be little, if any, interference from the North. Johnson also thought the northern federal government had no business making decisions for the southern states without first restoring their representation in Congress. His goal in Reconstruction was to put an end to southern aristocracy and return power to the common citizen. Congress, on the other hand, saw the rebel states as conquered provinces that deserved punishment for betraying the nation. The elected officials of Congress felt that they had the right to dictate the terms by which southern states would be restored to the Union, including the status of freed slaves and the shape of local governments.

In the late spring of 1865, the House of Representatives and the Senate adjourned and were not scheduled to return until the fall session. Although he faced criticism, the President decided to act on Reconstruction himself. He ignored calls for a special session of Congress and immediately signed two proclamations forming the basis of his plan for Reconstruction. The first restored citizenship to any southerner who would swear allegiance to the United States. The second instructed all former Confederate states to hold constitutional conventions to appoint new governments, which diluted the power of Confederate politicians by excluding them from the process. Additionally, Johnson proclaimed all southern states were to repeal any legal provisions related to its secession, repay all accrued war debts, and ratify the Thirteenth Amendment eliminating slavery.

The South welcomed Johnson's plan, seeing it as a quick and reasonable method of reintegration into the Union. But the opinions of radical Republicans in the northern states, who controlled the vote in Congress, were decidedly different. They were outraged. Northerners heard reports that the South was quickly returning to the antebellum status quo. White plantation owners were abusing the newly freed black Americans, in many cases restoring the spirit, if not the letter, of slavery. Some of the southern states enacted "black codes" that prohibited freed slaves from owning land, banned them from testifying against whites in court, and, in some cases, even permitted plantation owners to use forced labor. Northern Republicans also heard that the same men who'd founded the Confederacy now controlled government patronage and were rebuilding their political power base. Johnson's critics blamed him for squandering all of the Union's hard-won gains.

An angry Congress reconvened that December with Republicans determined to take charge of the Reconstruction process. First, they refused to seat the newly elected members from the southern states. Then they formed a committee of fifteen to evaluate President Johnson's progress and recommend different legislation based on its findings. A bitter struggle raged between the executive and legislative branches of government, one that would define Andrew Johnson's presidency and ultimately lead to his impeachment.

Congress began nullifying the President's plan piece by piece. They instituted military rule to the secessionist states. Then the House created legislation to extend the life of the Freedmen's Bureau, an agency created by Abraham Lincoln to provide schools, medical aid, and resettlement programs to southern blacks as a step towards integrating them into society. Most took it for granted that Johnson would approve the bureau's extension. Instead, he vetoed the bill on February 18, 1866, stating that the Freedmen's Bureau was a corrupt agency of "immense patronage" and was only an attempt to extend federal authority beyond its constitutional mandate. The veto became the first of twenty-nine, far more than any of Johnson's predecessors.

To many, Johnson, a native Tennessean, was simply displaying southern racist tendencies. The President criticized Congress for unconstitutionally writing laws extending benefits for the blacks the government didn't give to "our own people," as he characterized white Americans. He also scolded Congress for unconstitutionally making laws even though eleven states remained unrepresented. The president, Johnson claimed, was elected by the entire country and thus was better able to act in the national interest than those elected in a single district.

Republicans were enraged at the language, which they found arrogant, used in the president's veto. They promptly attempted an override but failed by two votes when a few senators went against the majority, refusing to override a presidential decision. The Freedman's Bureau ended.

Although President Johnson honestly believed the bureau unconstitutionally infringed on states' rights to manage their own internal affairs, the veto was part of a broader political strategy. Johnson hoped that by provoking the more radical Republicans in Congress, he could cause a split between them and the more moderate members of the party. He planned to then align moderate Republicans with southern Democrats in a coalition supporting him in the 1868 election.

In March, Congress passed the Civil Rights Act guaranteeing equal protection under the law for all citizens, regardless of race, creed, or color. Many Republicans viewed the legislation as an expression of the principles that caused the war, and its passage would be the basis of Reconstruction in the South. Everyone expected Johnson to sign the bill. For him to do otherwise would be political suicide. As one senator noted, "We all feel that the most important interests are at stake . . . . If the President vetoes the Civil Rights Bill, I believe that we shall be obliged to draw our swords for a fight and throw away the scabbards."

But Johnson did veto the bill, ending any possibility of a compromise between him and Congress. The radicals declared war and pledged to override Johnson's veto.

Congress underscored its defiance of the President later that year when it passed approval of the text of the Fourteenth Amendment, which would make the main portions of the vetoed Civil Rights Act part of the Constitution. The Amendment was forwarded to every state in the Union for ratification. Ironically, the only state that accepted it was Tennessee, Johnson's adopted home state. Un-ratified, the Fourteenth Amendment became fodder for debate in the 1866 midterm congressional elections.

Republicans swept the elections, sending a bitter message to the White House. When the new Congress convened in Washington, they wasted no time in working control away from Johnson in matters involving Reconstruction. The Republican Party effectively divided the South into military zones, denied Southern states Congressional representation, and restored martial law with the Military Reconstruction Act of 1867. The Republican-controlled Congress demanded Southern states hold new conventions, reform local governments, ratify the Fourteenth Amendment, and include all black males in the process before re-entry into the Union would be considered. Johnson was outraged by the action. He retaliated with systematic resistance to the Reconstruction policy by publicly undermining Republican efforts and using his powers as Commander in Chief to remand orders and replace military officers who were loyal to the Republicans.

The Republican radical majority fought back by targeting the presidential powers that made Johnson's resistance possible. They passed the Army Appropriations Act requiring the President to send all military orders through its chief commander, General Ulysses S. Grant. By doing so, Congress was able to circumvent the Commander-In-Chief by ordering policy compliance, despite Johnson's wishes. The power struggle grew.

In February of 1867 Congress took another shot at the President by enacting the Tenure in Office Act, which denied the President from firing or replacing any appointee without Senate approval. This meant that Johnson was denied the privilege of making changes in his Cabinet without Congressional approval. Three of

Johnson's Cabinet members had already resigned over disputes with Johnson's policies. The Republicans in Congress feared Secretary of War Edwin Stanton, a Lincoln appointee and harsh Johnson critic, was next. The Tenure in Office Act effectively saved Stanton's job, preventing Johnson from putting a political ally in the post. The wick on the stick of dynamite burned down between President Johnson and the Republican majority in Congress.

Before challenging the Tenure in Office Act, Johnson waited for Congress's summer recess. Then he fired Stanton and appointed moderate Republican U.S. Grant, a reluctant candidate, as Secretary of War. Johnson forced a showdown: if Congress would not approve Stanton's dismissal, the President would challenge the constitutionality of the Tenure in Office Act in the courts. If Congress backed down, Johnson won a major political battle while removing a nuisance from his administration.

Johnson, however, underestimated the level of contempt with which the Republicans held him, as well as the level of outrage Stanton's firing would trigger. Radical Republicans discussed impeachment as early as the 1866 election, when they garnered the necessary majorities in the House and Senate. Even so, all but the most radical of Republicans feared stepping into the arena of impeachment.

Ohio Representative James M. Ashley, an avowed Johnson enemy, had tried repeatedly to bring articles of impeachment since March 1867. Ashley went so far as to accuse Johnson of numerous abuses of presidential power and corruption. He even suggested the President was an agent of the South and that Lincoln's murder was part of a scheme to put Johnson in the White House and thereby subvert Republican plans for Reconstruction. No proof ever came to light regarding these charges, but a number of Americans believed them.

One of Ashley's impeachment motions finally made it through the House Judiciary Committee by a vote of five to four but was rejected on the House floor in a vote of one hundred and eight to

Roorbacked

A PERSONAL ATTACK ON CANDIDATES INSTEAD OF issues seems to be an enduring trait of the American presidential campaign. The election of 1844 pitted the often-a-candidate-never-a-winner Henry Clay of the Whig Party against the last of the Jackson Democrats, dark horse candidate James K. "Young Hickory" Polk.

Polk's camp threw the first mud ball when they claimed Henry Clay was known to have broken all of the Ten Commandments and resided in a Washington, D.C., brothel. The Whigs quickly fired back by portraying Polk as a cruel slave owner in hopes the story would enrage abolitionist Democrats, who would cast their votes for Clay.

On August 21, 1844, the abolitionist newspaper the *Chronicle* of Ithaca, New York, published segments of "Roorback's Tour" through the Southern and Western States in the Year 1836. The extracts were supposedly authored by Baron von Roorback, a German tourist. The *Chronicle* printed an excerpt from the book describing a slave trader's camp in Tennessee. The expert included the snippet, "Forty of these unfortunate beings had been purchased, I was told, by the Honorable J.K. Polk, the present speaker of the House of Representatives; the mark of the branding iron, with the initials of his name on their shoulders distinguishing them from the rest." Other abolitionist papers picked up on the story and printed it as well.

Democrats quickly picked up on the fraud and sought immediate retractions. In fact, Polk's name never even appeared in the book. The plot seems to have backfired on candidate Henry Clay, himself a slave owner from Kentucky, and he was criticized for the hypocrisy. The scandal coined a new term in American politics—Roorback—which refers to a lie spread for political effect. ✪

fifty-seven. Johnson mistook the floor vote as a sign of confidence in his Reconstruction plan and turned up the tempo by ousting radical Republican military officers and countermanding their orders. He also began to encourage southern opposition to the Republicans' Reconstruction ideas.

Meanwhile, the legislature invoked the Tenure in Office Act and reinstated Edwin Stanton as Secretary of War. Johnson promptly fired him again and in doing so violated the letter of the law for the first time during his administration. Obviously, he knew what he was doing. It was as if he was daring Congress to impeach. Congress accepted the challenge on February 24, 1868, when Pennsylvania Representative John Covode introduced a resolution to impeach on the House floor. Even before the formal articles were prepared, the full House voted one hundred and twenty-six to forty-seven to impeach.

The Constitution directs that cases of impeachment be indicted in the House and tried in the Senate, with the judge being the Chief Justice of the Supreme Court. Impeachable offenses are described as "Treason, Bribery, or other High Crimes and Misdemeanors." Johnson was charged with eleven articles of impeachment. Beside the charge of violating the Tenure in Office Act by illegally canning Stanton, the House charged Johnson with attempting to induce a Union general to accept orders in violation of the Army Appropriations Act. Others included denying Congressional authority, attempting to bring members of Congress "into disgrace," and speaking disrespectfully of Congress "in a loud voice."

The defense's toughest job was convincing the temperamental President to keep his mouth shut. The defense contended that the Tenure in Office Act didn't apply to Secretary Stanton's dismissal because Johnson was not president when Stanton was appointed. Then, in an apparent contradiction, the defense maintained Johnson had violated the Tenure Act simply to get the matter before the courts for judgment of constitutionality.

Republican prosecutors countered by mentioning that the Constitution provided the president with veto powers if he disagreed with proposed legislation—but the Constitution also granted Congress the power to override a veto. The prosecutors insisted the President was obligated to enforce the law whether or not he agreed with it. They said Johnson had deliberately neglected his constitutional duty and threatened the balance of power. The President, they claimed, like any other American, is legally liable for his actions. In President Johnson's case, that meant impeachment.

Public opinion swayed dramatically against Johnson, which shocked him. His plan to form a coalition of moderate Republicans and Democrats to win the November election disappeared before his eyes. His political future was all but dead. His attorneys began quietly suggesting to moderates that, if acquitted, President Johnson would serve the rest of his term and then fade away.

On May 16, 1868, the Senate voted on the first article of impeachment. The tally was thirty-five to nineteen, one vote short of the necessary two-thirds to convict. Ten days later, the same thing happened in the votes on the next two articles. One vote from impeachment on the first three articles, the Senate adjourned, closing the proceedings.

Andrew Johnson became the lamest of lame duck presidents. He did indeed serve his remaining ten months in office quietly, dutifully signing legislation the Republican Congress set before him. Reconstruction in the South resumed, undisputedly on Republican terms.

President Warren G. Harding

5

Teapot Doom

Warren G. Harding

JUST NORTH OF CASPER, WYOMING, A strange-looking natural rock formation towers seventy feet above the western horizon. It's called Teapot Rock because, until a 1962 tornado knocked off its spout, it was shaped like an old teapot. Because of its location, Teapot Rock, at least the "teapot" moniker, became synonymous with one of the most infamous presidential scandals in American history.

The story began right after the turn of the twentieth century with the beginning of a conservation movement in the American west. Conservationists were interested in preserving the country's natural resources—particularly forests, oil, and coal—for use by future generations. This notion didn't sit well with a contingent of Americans, including some politicians, who held onto an old idea that America's natural resources were inexhaustible. One of the latter was Secretary of the Interior Albert B. Fall. Born in Kentucky, Fall came from the New Mexico Territory by way of Texas. He was elected as one of the first Senators from New Mexico in 1918. In 1921, President Warren G. Harding selected Fall to serve as Secretary of the Interior.

In the American West, most land was still owned by the federal government. Unlike the East, where most natural resources were privately owned and use depended on supply and demand, exploiting natural resources was about the only way a man could earn big bucks out West. Albert B. Fall understood the immediate opportunity. He explained his stance once to a National Park Service official who'd asked him how his non-conservation views would affect his grandchildren:

> I'm surprised at you. You've had a good education. You know something about history. Every generation from Adam and Eve on down has lived better than the generation before. I don't know how succeeding generations will do it—maybe they'll use the energy of the sun or the sea waves—but they will live better than we do. I stand for opening up every resource.

Fall's view on conservation extended to several government oil reserves, including one at Teapot Dome, Wyoming. The reserves had been created after 1913 when the United States Navy committed to converting the U.S. fleet from coal to oil. The government

252

believed that in a war the oil fields in reserve could mean the difference between victory and defeat. But in 1920, Congress, many of whose members were acting under the influence of big oil money and lobbies, passed the Leasing Law allowing private exploitation for profit of minerals, including oil, on government land. The leasing law legislation appeared to make all the entities happy. Conservationists got leasing (as opposed to outright sales) as well as regulation designed to prevent waste. Oil companies got a valuable source of product and the opportunity to claim potential new oil fields. The legislation prevented monopolization by any single company. And both the federal government and cash-poor Western states got a share of the lease income.

There was a problem, however, with the naval reserve at Teapot Dome. Geologists feared the Teapot could be drained from newly opened oilfields in nearby Elk Hills and Salt Creek. Management of the leases and funding for federal oil fields fell under the Interior Department. The navy gained control of Elk Hills on June 4, 1920, with a naval appropriations bill that wrested the power from the Interior Department.

Enter President Warren G. Harding in 1921. Historians are split on why the Republican Party selected Harding as its 1920 presidential candidate. It's been suggested that big oil companies bought the Harding presidency. It's also true that certain powerful politicians wanted a weak leader in the White House, and Warren G. fit the bill.

Conservationists liked Harding's platform, which they helped write, on national natural resources. Leading conservationist Gifford Pinchot endorsed Harding and was consulted by the President-elect to suggest candidates for the post of Secretary of the Interior. By February 1921, though, Pinchot began to have doubts about his endorsement when he learned the new head of the Interior Department would be none other than Harding's old poker-playing buddy from the Senate, Albert Fall. "He has been with the exploitation

(left) Political shyster-turned-Interior-Secretary, Senator Albert Fall, a good ol' boy poker buddy of Warren Harding's, engineered a sweet deal for himself and his pals at the oil fields in Teapot, Wyoming. (above) The rock formation towering over the oil-rich land that gave Teapot Dome its name.

gang, but not a leader," Pinchot told a friend. He later wrote, "On the record, it would have been possible to pick a worse man for Secretary of Interior, but not altogether easy."

Pinchot's concern seemed justified when on May 31, 1921, President Harding issued an executive order transferring authority over the naval reserves from the Secretary of the Navy to the Secretary of the Interior. On July 12, six weeks later, Secretary Fall granted drilling rights at Elk Hills to millionaire Edward Doheny's Pan-American Petroleum and Transport Company. To this point, everything was legal and above board. Three oil companies placed bids on the contract, and Fall had taken the highest bid.

Then, in March of 1922, Washington lawyer and staunch conservationist Harry Slattery heard Albert Fall had just leased large tracts within Elk Hills to Pan-American Petroleum. Slattery contacted Senator Robert M. LaFollette, a friend of the conservationists, suggesting the Senate ask Secretary Fall to provide details about all leases on oil reserves. A little over a month later, Slattery wrote, "there has been a sudden change, we are fighting old Fall on the 'oil line'—particularly naval oil reserves." LaFollette was becoming equally suspicious, especially when he noticed that Navy officers who opposed the leasing were suddenly being transferred to distant posts.

On April 10 Slattery heard that Fall, just a couple of days before, had leased exclusive drilling rights for all of Teapot Dome to Henry Sinclair of Mammoth Oil. By April 14, the deal was front-page news in the *Wall Street Journal*.

By April 18, Fall had launched into damage control. He made a formal announcement of the Teapot Dome deal and provided the Senate with a copy of the contract. The lease appeared to be standard industry practice, but one portion seemed unusual. Royalties were not to be paid in cash or oil but in certificates redeemable to the Navy for oil products or oil storage tanks. Money would have been deposited in the Federal Treasury, and oil was useless to the Navy with nowhere to store it. The scheme provided the Navy with oil and storage. Two parts of the deal stunk to high heaven. There was no bidding on the contract—and all of the business went to Mammoth Oil. A week later, Fall announced a similar deal with Pan-American in the California oil reserves, except this one traded oil for oil exchange, storage tanks, and port facilities at the naval base at Pearl Harbor, Hawaii.

Odd as the deals seemed, they still gained little attention from the public. Senator LaFollette stayed on the case, however, managing to get a Senate resolution requiring the Interior Department to provide information about the leases. In late April he delivered a scathing speech on the Senate floor demanding an investigation as to why Mammoth Oil received favor "by the Government with a special privilege in value beyond the dreams of Croesus?" (Both leases were valued at over $100 million 1922 dollars.) The next day the Senate voted fifty-eight to zero to investigate.

The hearings began eighteen months after the Senate's approval of an investigation, a delay due mostly to Fall, who tried to overwhelm investigators with huge numbers of documents. By the first day of hearings on October 22, 1923, Albert Fall had left public office, his reputation still intact. Likewise, Warren G. Harding departed public office largely unscathed when he died unexpectedly on August 2.

Early days of the hearing were uneventful and, to some, boring and unnecessary. Albert Fall testified for two days, claiming the leasing of the naval oil reserve sites were vital to national defense. Neither the press nor most of the committee seemed impressed. Then in December, the lead investigator, Senator Thomas J. Walsh of Montana, a man known for his integrity, began to hear stories about "some significant land deals in New Mexico." That autumn, when other New Mexico ranchers suffered from a drought and low cattle prices, Citizen Fall found enough money to enlarge and improve his vast cattle ranch. Oilmen Edward Doheny of Pan-American and Henry Sinclair of Mammoth testified they hadn't given Fall any money. But Fall wasn't happy about the innuendo involving his ranch. He then made what he later described as the biggest mistake of his life. He wrote to Senator Walsh claiming that his sudden prosperity came from a $100,000 loan he procured from *Washington Post* publisher Edward B. McLean. By the end of December, some said Senator Walsh's investigation was "up against a stone wall." Then Walsh received a telegram inviting him to Palm Beach, Florida, for a visit with Ed McLean at his winter house.

McLean had confirmed the loan in an earlier correspondence to Walsh and the other members of the committee, adding he would

One for You, Two for Me

THE PRESIDENTIAL ELECTION OF 1876 IS CONSIDERED by many to be the most corrupt in American history. But Republican candidate Rutherford B. Hayes wasn't too upset when he went to bed on election night thinking he was a loser to Democrat Samuel Tilden. After all, Tilden's victory was already all over the front pages of newspapers across the country.

But Republican *New York Times* managing editor John Reid saw the possibility of a different spin on the election. After ensuring the *Times* printed a headline declaring the election was still very much in doubt, Reid began pulling strings for Hayes, proving it's not how many votes you get but how you count them.

Before the sun rose, Reid strolled over to Republican National Committee headquarters at the Fifth Avenue Hotel. There he found party chairman Zachariah Chandler apparently sleepy in defeat. Chandler woke up to Reid's, "If you will only keep your heads, there is no question of the election of President Hayes." Chandler threw the party reigns to Reid, who started working some political magic. Reid fired up the telegraph lines telling Republican workers in Florida, Louisiana, South Carolina, and Oregon that the election was still not over. Count every vote! The only glitch came when the telegraph operator told Reid the Republicans didn't have an account. No problem—the *New York Times* picked up the tab.

Reid's telegrams ultimately inspired Republicans to contest the vote in all those key battleground states. Months of bitter partisan wrestling for every single vote put the country on edge. Eventually a special electoral commission was appointed. The commission voted along party lines and, the winner was . . . Rutherford B. Hayes, of course. Ah, the Power of the Press. ✪

be happy to talk to the committee if they came to Florida. Walsh agreed the investigation was going nowhere, but he decided to visit McLean before ending the inquiry. There, on January 12, the Senator was "dumbfounded" to learn McLean now denied lending Fall any money.

Fall also happened to be vacationing in Palm Beach at the time. Walsh used the opportunity to see Fall in person for an explanation. The former politician admitted he hadn't accepted a loan from McLean, but he insisted the cash he used for ranch enhancements was "in no way" connected to Mammoth Oil. Technically, Fall told the truth. The $100,000 came from Doheny and Pan-American. Mammoth had provided Fall with $233,000 in Liberty bonds and only $36,000 in cash. Combined, Albert Fall had accepted about $409,000, a staggering sum in 1923, from the two companies.

Almost overnight, the dull debate over oil and government policy transformed into a titillating tale of bribery, perjury, and cover-up involving government officials and two of the richest oil companies in America. Mounds of litigation involving payoffs and oil company interests ensued. In June of 1925, a Wyoming judge declared Henry Sinclair's Mammoth Oil lease on Teapot Dome still valid. The judge opined that the government was unable to submit direct proof of Sinclair and Mammoth's $233,000 payoff to ex-Secretary Fall. The government appealed and won. Sinclair appealed to the Supreme Court, where he lost on October 10, 1927.

Unsatisfied, Walsh persisted like a pit bull on the trail of the $233,000. He finally used serial numbers to trace the money back to a Canadian corporation called Continental Trading Company, which had laundered the money to enrich its investors, including Henry Sinclair, by buying oil at $1.50 a barrel and immediately selling it for $1.75 a barrel without ever even seeing the oil. The scam netted a few select investors over two million dollars in less than a year and a half, after which, the corporation was promptly liquidated and its records destroyed. Again, Walsh had little or nothing to go on. Anybody who knew about Continental Trading was either out of the country or claiming ignorance. But Walsh refused to give up and went after M.T. Everhart, Fall's son-in-law, who invoked his right not to testify, citing self-incrimination privilege.

But Walsh wouldn't give up. He convinced Congress to alter the statute of limitations so Everhart's testimony no longer could be used against him. January 24, 1928, four years after the original inquiry, new Teapot Dome hearings began. The first witness, M.T. Everhart, testifying under duress, admitted that in May of 1922 Mammoth Oil's Henry Sinclair had given him $233,000 in Liberty bonds that he had passed on to Albert Fall.

Criminal prosecutions, with mixed results, followed for Fall, Doheny, and Sinclair. All three were indicted on charges of conspiracy and bribery in June 1924. In November 1926, a jury exonerated Fall and Doheny on conspiracy charges. Seven months later, Fall and Sinclair went on trial for similar charges, but a mistrial occurred when Sinclair was found to be tampering with the jury. He spent six months for the infraction. Sinclair's second conspiracy trial happened in April 1928. Although prosecutor's proved his $233,000 payoff to Fall, the jury found him innocent.

That October, Albert Fall, now in ill health, was tried and found guilty of bribery. He was sentenced to one year in prison. By March, Doheny faced the same judge in the same courtroom, accused of offering the bribe that Fall accepted. A jury found him innocent.

Despite years of investigation, mountains of evidence, and the prosecutor's best efforts, Albert Fall is the only man to have served time for the Teapot Dome Scandal. Senator George Norris of Nebraska may have summed up the whole affair when he sarcastically quipped, "We ought to pass a law that no man worth $100 million should be tried for a crime."

For his part, or the lack of it, Warren G. Harding, long dead and far after the fact, is still known as the president who owns The Teapot Dome Scandal.

Dick and Pat Nixon in the early "I am not a crook" days.

6

Go Checkers! Save Dick!

Richard Nixon

IN 1952 RICHARD NIXON BECAME THE subject of an investigation (his first time!) for maintaining a slush fund and accepting gifts in office. Nixon was the Republican ticket's candidate for vice president. Instead of arguing through lawyers, the courts, or political outlets, Nixon took his case right to the American people via the relatively new medium of television. What became known as the "Checkers Speech" is regarded as one of the best political public relations spin speeches in modern American history.

It helped elect Eisenhower president and not only kept Dick Nixon on the ticket, but was a springboard of sorts to his political future. Here's the speech in its entirety. Note Nixon's use of the "average American family" and "common man" images to make his case as well as his righteous indignation (very much tempered, of course). He also doesn't miss a chance to backhand the current administration, using his self-defense to get in a dig or two. The speech provides a glimpse into the president who would use similar tactics when under fire for the Watergate scandal twenty years later.

My Fellow Americans,

I come before you tonight as a candidate for the vice-presidency and as a man whose honesty and integrity has been questioned.

Now, the usual political thing to do when charges are made against you is to either ignore them or to deny them without giving details. I believe we have had enough of that in the United States, particularly with the present administration in Washington, D.C.

To me, the office of the vice-presidency of the United States is a great office, and I feel that the people have got to have confidence in the integrity of the men who run for that office and who might attain them.

I have a theory, too, that the best and only answer to a smear or an honest misunderstanding of the facts is to tell the truth. And that is why I am here tonight. I want to tell you my side of the case.

I am sure that you have read the charges, and you have heard it, that I, Senator Nixon, took $18,000 from a group of my supporters.

Now, was that wrong? And let me say that it was wrong. I am saying it, incidentally, that it was wrong, just not illegal, because it isn't a question of whether it was legal or illegal, that isn't enough. The question is, was it morally wrong? I say that it was morally wrong if any of that $18,000 went to Senator Nixon, for my personal use. I say that it was morally wrong if it was secretly given and secretly handled.

And I say that it was morally wrong if any of the contributors got special favors for the contributions that they made.

And to answer those questions let me say this—not a cent of the $18,000 or any other money of that type ever went to me for my personal use. Every penny of it was used to pay for political expenses that I did not think should be charged to the taxpayers of the United States.

It was not a secret fund. As a matter of fact, when I was on *Meet the Press*—some of you may have seen it last Sunday—Peter Edson came up to me after the program, and he said, "Dick, what about this fund we hear about?" And I said, "Well, there is no secret about it. Go out and see Dana Smith who was the administrator of the fund," and I gave him his address. And I said you will find that the purpose of the fund simply was to defray political expenses that I did not feel should be charged to the government.

And third, let me point out, and I want to make this particularly clear, that no contributor to this fund, no contributor to any of my campaigns, has ever received any consideration that he would not have received as an ordinary constituent.

I just don't believe in that, and I can say that never, while I have been in the Senate of the United States, as far as the people that contributed to this fund are concerned, have I made a telephone call to an agency, nor have I gone down to an agency on their behalf.

And the records will show that—the records which are in the hands of the administration.

Well, then, some of you will say, and rightly, "Well, what did you use the fund for, Senator? Why did you have to have it?"

Let me tell you in just a word how a Senate office operates. First of all, the Senator gets $15,000 a year in salary. He gets enough money to pay for one trip a year, a round trip, that is, for himself, and his family between his home and Washington, D.C. And then he gets an allowance to handle the people that work in his office to handle his mail.

And the allowance for my State of California is enough to hire thirteen people. And let me say, incidentally, that this allowance is not paid to the Senator. It is paid directly to the individuals, that the Senator puts on his payroll, but all of these people and all of these allowances are for strictly official business—business, for example, when a constituent writes in and wants you to go down to the Veteran's Administration and get some information about his GI policy—items of that type, for example. But there are other expenses that are not covered by the government. And I think I can best discuss those expenses by asking you some questions.

Do you think that when I or any other Senator makes a political speech, has it printed, should charge the printing of that speech and the mailing of that speech to the taxpayers?

Do you think, for example, when I or any other Senator makes a trip to his home state to make a purely political speech that the cost of that trip should be charged to the taxpayers?

Do you think when a Senator makes political broadcasts or political television broadcasts, radio or television, that the expense of those broadcasts should be charged to the taxpayers?

I know what your answer is. It is the same answer that audiences give me whenever I discuss this particular problem.

The answer is no. The taxpayers should not be required to finance items which are not official business but which are primarily political business.

Well, then the question arises, you say, "Well, how do you pay for these and how can you do it legally?" And there are several ways that it can be done, incidentally, and it is done legally in the United States Senate and in the Congress.

The first way is to be a rich man. So I couldn't use that.

Another way that is used is to put your wife on the payroll. Let me say, incidentally, that my opponent, my opposite number for the vice-presidency on the Democratic ticket, does have his wife on the payroll and has had her on his payroll for the past ten years. Now let me just say this—That is his business, and I am not critical of him for doing that. You will have to pass judgment on that particular point, but I have never done that for this reason: I have found that there are so many deserving stenographers and secretaries in Washington that needed the work that I just didn't feel it was right to put my wife on the payroll—My wife sitting over there.

She is a wonderful stenographer. She used to teach stenography and she used to teach shorthand in high school. That was when I met her. And I can tell you folks that she has worked many hours on Saturdays and Sundays in my office, and she has done a fine job, and I am proud to say tonight that in the six years I have been in the Senate of the United States, Pat Nixon has never been on the government payroll.

What are the other ways that these finances can be taken care of? Some who are lawyers, and I happen to be a lawyer, continue to practice law, but I haven't been able to do that.

I am so far away from California and I have been so busy with my senatorial work that I have not engaged in any legal practice, and, also, as far as law practice is concerned, it seemed to me that the relationship between an attorney and the client was so personal that you couldn't possibly represent a man as an attorney and then have an unbiased view when he presented his case to you in the event that he had one before government.

And so I felt that the best way to handle these necessary political expenses of getting my message to the American people and the speeches I made—the speeches I had printed for the most part concerned this one message of exposing this administration, the Communism in it, the corruption in it—the only way I could do that was to accept the aid which people in my home state of California, who contributed to my campaign and who continued to make these contributions after I was elected, were glad to make.

And let me say that I am proud of the fact that not one of them has ever asked me for a special favor. I am proud of the fact that not one of them has ever asked me to vote on a bill other than my own conscience would dictate. And I am proud of the fact that the taxpayers by subterfuge or otherwise have never paid one dime for expenses which I thought were political and should not be charged to the taxpayers.

Let me say, incidentally, that some of you may say, "Well, that is all right, Senator, that is your explanation, but have you got any proof?" And I would like to tell you this evening that just an hour ago we received an independent audit of this entire fund. I suggested to Governor Sherman Adams, who is the chief of staff of the Eisenhower campaign, that an independent audit and legal report be obtained, and I have that audit in my hand.

It is an audit made by Price Waterhouse and Company firm, and the legal opinion by Gibson, Dunn, and Crutcher, lawyers in Los Angeles, the biggest law firm, and incidentally, one of the best ones in Los Angeles.

I am proud to report to you tonight that this audit and legal opinion is being forwarded to General Eisenhower and I would like to read to you the opinion that was prepared by Gibson, Dunn, and Crutcher, based on all the pertinent laws, and statutes, together with the audit report prepared by the certified public accountants.

It is our conclusion that Senator Nixon did not obtain any financial gain from the collection and disbursement of the funds by Dana Smith; that Senator Nixon did not violate any federal or state law by reason of the operation of the fund; and that neither the portion of the fund paid by Dana Smith directly to third persons, nor the portion paid to Senator Nixon, to reimburse him for office expenses, constituted income in a sense which was either reportable or taxable as income under income tax laws.

Signed—Gibson, Dunn, & Crutcher, by Elmo Conley

That is not Nixon speaking, but it is an independent audit which was requested because I want the American people to know all the facts and I am not afraid of having independent people go in and check the facts, and that is exactly what they did.

But then I realized that there are still some who may say, and rightly so—and let me say that I recognize that some will continue to smear regardless of what the truth may be—but that there has been understandably, some honest misunderstanding on this matter, and there are some that will say, "Well, maybe you were able, Senator, to fake the thing. How can we believe what you say—after all, is there a possibility that maybe you got some sums in cash? Is there a possibility that you might have feathered your own nest?" And so now, what I am going to do—and incidentally this is unprecedented in the history of American politics—I am going at this time to give to this television and radio audience, a complete financial history, everything I have earned, everything I have spent and everything I own, and I want you to know the facts.

I will have to start early, I was born in 1913. Our family was one of modest circumstances, and most of my early life was spent in a store out in East Whittier. It was a grocery store, one of those family enterprises.

The only reason we were able to make it go was because my mother and dad had five boys, and we all worked in the store. I worked my way through college, and, to a great extent, through law school. And then in 1940, probably the best thing that ever happened to me happened. I married Pat, who is sitting over here.

We had a rather difficult time after we were married, like so many of the young couples who might be listening to us. I practiced law. She continued to teach school.

Then, in 1942, I went into the service. Let me say that my service record was not a particularly unusual one. I went to the South Pacific. I guess I'm entitled to a couple of battle stars. I got a couple of letters of commendation. But I was just there when the bombs were falling. And then I returned. I returned to the United States, and in 1946, I ran for Congress. When we came out of the war—Pat and I—Pat during the war had worked as a stenographer, and in a bank, and as an economist for a government agency—and when we came out, the total of our savings, from both my law practice, her teaching and all the time I was in the war, the total for that entire period was just less than $10,000—every cent of that, incidentally, was in government bonds—well, that's where we start, when I go into politics.

Now, whatever I earned since I went into politics—well, here it is. I jotted it down. Let me read the notes.

First of all, I have had my salary as a Congressman and as a Senator.

Second, I have received a total in this past six years of $1,600 from estates which were in my law firm at the time that I severed my connection with it. And, incidentally, as I said before, I have not engaged in any legal practice, and have not accepted any fees from business that came into the firm after I went into politics.

And then, unfortunately, we

I have made an average of approximately $1,500 a year from nonpolitical speaking engagements and lectures.

And then, unfortunately, we have inherited little money. Pat sold her interest in her father's estate for $3,000, and I inherited $1,500 from my grandfather. We lived rather modestly.

For four years we lived in an apartment in Parkfairfax, Alexandria, Virginia. The rent was $80 a month. And we saved for a time when we could buy a house. Now that was what we took in.

What did we do with this money? What do we have today to show for it? This will surprise you because it is so little. I suppose as standards generally go of people in public life.

First of all, we've got a house in Washington, which cost $41,000 and on which we owe $20,000. We have a house in Whittier, California, which cost $13,000 and on which we owe $3,000. My folks are living there at the present time.

I have just $4,000 in life insurance, plus my GI policy which I have never been able to convert, and which will run out in two years.

I have no life insurance whatever on Pat. I have no life insurance on our two youngsters, Patricia and Julie.

I own a 1950 Oldsmobile car. We have our furniture. We have no stocks and bonds of any type. We have no interest, direct or indirect, in any business. Now that is what we have. What do we owe?

Well, in addition to the mortgages, the $20,000 mortgage on the house in Washington and the $10,000 mortgage on the house in Whittier, I owe $4,000 to the Riggs Bank in Washington, D.C. with an interest at 4 percent.

I owe $3,500 to my parents, and the interest on that loan, which I pay regularly, because it is a part of the savings they made through

have inherited little money.

the years they were working so hard—I pay regularly 4 percent interest. And then I have a $500 loan, which I have on my life insurance. Well, that's about it. That's what we have. And that's what we owe. It isn't very much.

But Pat and I have the satisfaction that every dime that we have got is honestly ours.

I should say this, that Pat doesn't have a mink coat. But she does have a respectable Republican cloth coat, and I always tell her she would look good in anything.

One other thing I probably should tell you, because if I don't they will probably be saying this about me, too. We did get something, a gift, after the election.

A man down in Texas heard Pat on the radio mention the fact

that our two youngsters would like to have a dog, and, believe it or not, the day before we left on this campaign trip we got a message from Union Station in Baltimore, saying they had a package for us. We went down to get it. You know what it was?

It was a little cocker spaniel dog, in a crate that he had sent all the way from Texas, black and white, spotted, and our little girl Tricia, the six year old, named it Checkers.

And you know, the kids, like all kids, loved the dog, and I just want to say this, right now, that regardless of what they say about it, we are going to keep it.

It isn't easy to come before a nation-wide audience and bare your life, as I have done. But I want to say some things before I conclude, that I think most of you will agree on.

Mr. Mitchell, the Chairman of the Democratic National Committee, made this statement that if a man couldn't afford to be in the United States Senate, he shouldn't run for Senate. And I just want to make my position clear.

I don't agree with Mr. Mitchell when he says that only a rich man should serve his government in the United States Senate or Congress. I don't believe that represents the thinking of the Democratic Party, and I know it doesn't represent the thinking of the Republican Party.

I believe that it's fine that a man like Governor Stevenson, who inherited a fortune from his father, can run for president. But I also feel that it is essential in this country of ours that a man of modest means can also run for president, because, you know—remember Abraham Lincoln, you remember what he said—"God must have loved the common people, he made so many of them."

And now I'm going to suggest some courses of conduct.

First of all, you have read in the papers about other funds. Now, Mr. Stevenson apparently had a couple—one of them in which a group of business people paid and helped to supplement the salaries of state employees. Here is where the money went directly into their pockets, and I think that what Mr. Stevenson should do should be to come before the American people, as I have, give the names of the people that contributed to that fund, give the names of the people who put this money into their pockets, at the same time that they were receiving money from their state government and see what favors, if any, they gave out for that.

I don't condemn Mr. Stevenson for what he did, but until the facts are in, there is a doubt that would be raised. And as far as Mr. Sparkman is concerned, I would suggest the same thing. He's had his wife on the payroll. I don't condemn him for that, but I think that he should come before the American people and indicate what outside sources of income he has had. I would suggest that under the circumstances both Mr. Sparkman and Mr. Stevenson should come before the American people, as I have, and make a complete financial statement as to their financial history, and if they don't, it will be an admission that they have something to hide.

And I think you will agree with me—because, folks, remember, a man that's to be President of the United States, a man that is to be Vice President of the United States, must have the confidence of all the people. And that's why I'm doing what I'm doing. And that is why I suggest that Mr. Stevenson and Mr. Sparkman, if they are under attack, that should be what they are doing.

Now let me say this: I know this is not the last of the smears. In spite of my explanation tonight, other smears will be made. Others have been made in the past. And the purpose of the smears, I know, is this—to silence me, to make me let up.

Well, they just don't know who they are dealing with. I'm going to tell you this: I remember in the dark days of the Hiss trial some of the same columnists, some of the same radio commentators who are attacking me now and misrepresenting my position, were violently opposing me at the time I was after Alger Hiss. But I continued to fight because I knew I was right, and I can say to this great television and radio audience that I have no apologies to the American people

PRESIDENTIAL PECCADILLOES

for my part in putting Alger Hiss where he is today. And as far as this is concerned, I intend to continue to fight.

Why do I feel so deeply? Why do I feel that in spite of the smears, the misunderstanding, the necessity for a man to come up here and bare his soul? And I want to tell you why.

Because, you see, I love my country. And I think my country is in danger. And I think the only man that can save America at this time is the man that's running for president, on my ticket, Dwight Eisenhower.

You say, why do I think it is in danger? And I say look at the record. Seven years of the Truman-Acheson administration, and what's happened? Six hundred million people lost to Communists.

And a war in Korea in which we have lost 117,000 American casualties, and I say that those in the State Department that made the mistakes which caused that war and which resulted in those losses should be kicked out of the State Department just as fast as we can get them out of there.

You wouldn't trust the man who

And let me say that I know Mr. Stevenson won't do that because he defends the Truman policy, and I know that Dwight Eisenhower will do that, and he will give America the leadership that it needs.

Take the problem of corruption. You have read about the mess in Washington. Mr. Stevenson can't clean it up because he was picked by the man, Truman, under whose administration the mess was made.

You wouldn't trust the man who made the mess to clean it up. That is Truman. And by the same token you can't trust the man who was picked by the man who made the mess to clean it up and that's Stevenson. And so I say, Eisenhower—who owes nothing to Truman, nothing to the big city bosses—he is the man who can clean up the mess in Washington.

Take Communism. I say as far as that subject is concerned the danger is greater to America. In the Hiss case they got the secrets which enabled them to break the American secret State Department code.

They got secrets in the atomic bomb case which enabled them to get the secret of the atomic bomb five years before they would have gotten it by their own devices. And I say that any man who called the Alger Hiss case a red herring isn't fit to be president of the United States.

I say that a man who, like Mr. Stevenson, has pooh-poohed and ridiculed the Communist threat in the United States—he has accused us, that they have attempted to expose the Communists, of looking for Communists in the Bureau of Fisheries and Wildlife. I say that a man who says that isn't qualified to be president of the United States.

And I say that the only man who can lead us into this fight to rid the government of both those who are Communists and those who

made the mess to clean it up.

have corrupted this government is Eisenhower, because General Eisenhower, you can be sure, recognizes the problem, and knows how to handle it.

Let me say this, finally. This evening I want to read to you just briefly excerpts from a letter that I received, a letter, which after all this is over, no one can take away from us. It reads as follows:

Dear Senator Nixon,

Since I am only 19 years of age, I can't vote in this presidential election, but believe me if I could, you and General Eisenhower would certainly get my vote. My husband is in the Fleet Marines in Korea. He is in the front lines. And we have a two-month-old son he has never seen. And I feel confident that with great Americans like you and General Eisenhower in the White House, lonely Americans like myself will be united with their loved ones now in Korea. I only pray to God that you won't be too late. Enclosed is a small check to help you with your campaign. Living on $85 a month, it is all I can do.

Folks, it is a check for $10, and it is one that I shall never cash. And let me just say this: We hear a lot about prosperity these days, but I say why can't we have prosperity built on peace, rather than prosperity built on war? Why can't we have prosperity and an honest government in Washington, D.C. at the same time?

Believe me, we can. And Eisenhower is the man that can lead the crusade to bring us that kind of prosperity.

And now, finally, I know that you wonder whether or not I am going to stay on the Republican ticket or resign. Let me say this: I don't believe that I ought to quit, because I am not a quitter. And, incidentally, Pat is not a quitter. After all, her name is Patricia Ryan and she was born on St. Patrick's Day, and you know the Irish never quit.

But the decision, my friends, is not mine. I would do nothing that would harm the possibilities of Dwight Eisenhower to become president of the United States. And for that reason I am submitting to the Republican National Committee tonight through this television broadcast the decision which it is theirs to make. Let them decide whether my position on the ticket will help or hurt. And I am going to ask you to help them decide. Wire and write the Republican National Committee whether you think I should stay on or whether I should get off. And whatever their decision, I will abide by it.

But let me just say this last word. Regardless of what happens, I am going to continue this fight. I am going to campaign up and down America until we drive the crooks and the Communists and those that defend them out of Washington, and remember, folks, Eisenhower is a great man. Folks, he is a great man, and a vote for Eisenhower is a vote for what is good for America.

Richard M. Nixon - September 23, 1952

Man's Best Friend

AND SPEAKING OF DOGS, IT'S BEEN SAID WARREN G. Harding treated his dog better than his wife—or girlfriends. Harding loved his dog, Laddie Boy, so much he arranged to have him assigned Dog License #1 and even threw him a birthday party in the White House rose garden, where Laddie Boy was served cake made of dog biscuits frosted with icing.

When Harding heard the sad tale of a canine being smuggled into the country illegally that was ordered put to sleep by a Pennsylvania judge, he interceded by requesting a reprieve from Pennsylvania's governor. A pardon was granted.

When Harding the newspaperman-turned-president passed on to his final reward in 1923, the Newsboy's Association of America, of which Harding was a member, decided to build a Laddie Boy statue in the late president's honor. The association asked every newsboy in America to donate a penny. One hundred and three pounds of pennies were collected and melted down to produce a bronze Laddie Boy statue. You can visit Laddie Boy today at the Smithsonian Institute. ★

President Lyndon B. Johnson

7

The Bank Account as Big as Texas

PRESIDENT LYNDON JOHNSON CAME FROM humble beginnings. He was born on August 27, 1908, in Stonewall, Texas, in a poor neighborhood near the Pedernales River. He worked through his teen years, putting himself through Southwest Texas State Teacher's College, and he taught for a year after he graduated in 1930.

He found his way into politics when Texas Representative Richard Kleberg invited him to join his congressional staff. In Washington, Lyndon learned the ropes in the legislative process and developed an ardent admiration of President Franklin Roosevelt's New Deal. He enrolled at Georgetown Law School but dropped out when President Roosevelt appointed him Texas director of the National Youth Administration. He remained a man of modest means when he married Claudia Alta "Lady Bird" Taylor, the daughter of a successful Texas storekeeper and rancher, in November 1934. A few years later he began a successful career of his own in politics. By the time Jack Kennedy selected Johnson as his running mate in the 1960 presidential election, Johnson was a formidable force in Washington, and along the way he had become a millionaire.

In 1964, news reporters became curious about President Johnson's fortune, estimated at $14 million by then. Jack Kennedy inherited his wealth, but Johnson seemed to get rich while in office. Johnson's money initially came from Austin's radio-TV station KTBC. Lady Bird acquired KTBC in 1943 while her husband managed to secure FCC approval for the deal in an unprecedented three weeks.

KTBC held a monopoly over the large Austin market in that they were the only station in town. Speculation arose that Johnson used his political clout to garner favor with the FCC, an allegation that lent suspicion to the FCC's denial of broadcast licenses to potential competitors of KTBC in 1963. Johnson told the press he had no interest in the federally regulated business because everything was in his wife's and daughter's names. But when the August 1964 issue of *Life* magazine included an article estimating Johnson's family fortune at $14 million 1964 dollars, the President was forced to respond.

He released a professionally prepared audit of his worth, declaring assets of 3.5 million. He didn't say the figures used in the report were two decades old and not reflective of his current value. But the figures seemed to satisfy the American public, and the media couldn't prove any impropriety with the FCC. It's clear that LBJ went from rags to riches while living on the public nipple, but exactly how he did it has never been fully explained.

8

What's Bugging Dick?

GOOD OR BAD, RIGHT OR WRONG, Nixon's accomplishments as president are eclipsed by a scandal named after a Washington, D.C. hotel and office complex. But the real scandal didn't begin or end with a botched break-in at Democratic National Committee headquarters at the Watergate Hotel. What started as an amateur burglary grew into a criminal investigation that reached the highest levels of government, including the office of the president.

Watergate sprang from Nixon's obsessive determination for re-election in 1972. Ironically, a wide political schism in the Democratic Party probably ensured the incumbent's victory anyway—without any dirty tricks. The Democratic convention was contentious to say the least. Senator George McGovern of South Dakota became the Democratic candidate. McGovern's association with hippies and the anti-war movement made him controversial—too controversial for many traditional Democrats, who crossed party lines and helped President Nixon return to the White House in a landslide victory.

But, of course, his future as a shoo-in wasn't perfectly clear to Dick before the election, and he wasn't a man for taking chances. Instead, he winked at the sneaky, albeit illegal, campaign strategies dreamed up by his loyal followers on the White House staff and the Committee for the Re-election of the President (also known as "CREEP"). Richard Nixon's actions started a chain reaction of escalating scandal, starting with the pathetic burglary at the Watergate, and ultimately ending in the start of impeachment proceedings and his resignation.

At the end of Nixon's first term, the *New York Times* published a sketchy article about what became known as the "Pentagon Papers." A special assistant in the Pentagon's Office of International Security Affairs, Daniel Ellsberg, gave portions of a top-secret study of the history of the Vietnam War to the *Times* and the *Washington Post*. Ellsberg opposed the War, so he leaked the documents in hopes of enraging the American public to the point where they would demand its end. Instead, Ellsberg earned a place on the President's hate list.

Information leaks had occurred at the Pentagon before, and the administration was fed up. To quell the problem, Nixon and his advisors created a special clandestine unit to stop the security breaches. The unit, known as "the plumbers" because they plugged leaks, formed as a legally questionable partnership between members of the Nixon administration and their friends in the CIA. The plumbers started by burglarizing the Los Angeles office of Dr. Lewis Fielding, a psychiatrist who had once seen Ellsberg as a patient. The plumbers hoped to find Ellsberg's psychiatric file, which they thought might contain information the administration could use to disparage the informant before he was tried for espionage. They wanted to sway public opinion in hopes of ensuring a conviction. When they couldn't find Ellsberg's file in Fielding's office, the plumbers planned to break into Ellsberg's house, but they couldn't get approval from Washington.

The plot against Ellsberg didn't backfire until two years later, when it popped up during the Watergate investigation. Three mem-

The Watergate Hotel—home of the Democratic National Committee in the 1970s and the site of an amateur burglary that set Richard Nixon's presidency on its ear.

bers of the Nixon administration, including assistant for domestic affairs John D. Ehrlichman, were eventually convicted of conspiring to violate Daniel Ellsberg's civil rights. When the government conspiracy came to light, all of the charges against Ellsberg were dismissed. But the Ellsberg incident proved to be just a steppingstone in the constantly unraveling investigation of illicit and unconstitutional activities President Nixon and his aides were involved in.

The most sensational political scandal in modern American history started with an amateur-looking caper. In the early morning hours of June 17, 1972, a security guard at the Watergate Hotel found a fire exit open in the parking garage. The door's lock was taped open to prevent its locking. Not recognizing an old burglar's trick, the guard simply removed the tape and went about his business.

On his next round, the guard noticed the same door was again taped. He summoned the police, and minutes later three D.C. officers arrived on the scene. Climbing the stairs, they noticed every exit door in the stairwell was taped. On the sixth floor, they found the fire exit door out of the Democratic National Committee offices pried open. Searching the premises, the police discovered five men, dressed in business suits and wearing rubber surgical gloves, hiding in the dark in one of the offices.

The five men were arrested and booked on felony burglary and criminal tools charges. All five lied about their names when they were arrested, but their true identities soon came to light. Among the suspects, three were Cuban nationals, each with connections to the CIA, including the failed 1962 Bay of Pigs fiasco. Another was said to have CIA experience in training Cuban exiles in guerrilla warfare. The fifth man was identified as James W. McCord, an ex-CIA operative who was on the payroll of CREEP and as a security consultant for the Democratic National Committee. Other evidence soon implicated White House operatives E. Howard Hunt, Jr. and G. Gordon Liddy.

By all appearances, the perpetrators were leaving as much as they took. Filing cabinet drawers were open and a ceiling panel was out, suggesting the sophisticated photo equipment and eavesdropping devices the burglars possessed were intended to "bug" the DNC offices. Besides the cameras and tap equipment, police found a walkie-talkie, forty rolls of unexposed film, lock-picking tools, door jimmies, and three pen-sized canisters of tear gas. They also found $2,300 in sequentially numbered hundred-dollar bills in one of the suspect's hotel room. The cash would ultimately point investigators in the direction of the Oval Office.

A couple of days later, the *Washington Post* reported that one of those arrested in the Watergate burglary was a salaried security coordinator for President Nixon's re-election committee. James McCord, the article said, also happened to be an employee of the Republican National Committee. The White House promptly fired McCord, stating the administration was "surprised and dismayed" by his arrest.

As the investigation continued, *Washington Post* reporters Bob Woodward and Carl Bernstein chronicled new evidence of corruption and conspiracy on an almost-daily basis. The newsmen pursued the investigation doggedly until the end, earning them the Pulitzer Prize. During their investigation, Woodward and Bernstein had an anonymous informant from deep inside the government bureaucracy who confirmed or denied important information. Their source called himself "Deep Throat" to keep his identity hidden. And it remained hidden until 2005, when ex-FBI deputy director W. Mark Felt revealed that he was the man who assisted the *Washington Post* in breaking the Watergate story. Felt died on December 18, 2008, at the age of ninety-five.

With the Watergate break-in on front pages all over the country, White House aides scrambled to keep the burglary from being linked back to CREEP and the Nixon administration. In a cover-up attempt, Jeb Magruder, Nixon's deputy campaign director, John

Dean III, the White House general counsel, and other staff began destroying potential evidence and lying to investigators. White House Chief of Staff H.R. Haldeman designed a plan to dissuade the FBI's inquiry by suggesting it compromised a sensitive secret CIA operation. Later, FBI director Patrick Gray resigned after admitting that he had leaked FBI Watergate files to John Dean.

Meanwhile, Watergate co-conspirator E. Howard Hunt wanted a price for his silence, causing John Dean to say now-infamous lines to President Nixon: "We have a cancer within, close to the presidency, that's growing. It's growing daily. It's compounding. We're being blackmailed. People are going to start perjuring themselves very quickly." Dean went on to tell Nixon that Hunt's price might be as high as a million dollars, to which the President replied, "You could get the money. You could get it in cash. I know where it could be gotten."

"People are going to start perjuring

Lawyers for the Democratic National Committee said they were outraged by the break-in. Even if they were, they also saw the opportunity to turn the incident into a political jackpot. They quickly filed suit against CREEP seeking one million dollars in damages for its involvement in the scandal.

The first casualty of the Watergate affair was John Mitchell, Nixon's first attorney general. He resigned his post as Nixon's campaign manager on July 1, 1972, saying his wife, Martha, was making him quit politics. The *Washington Post* followed up on Mitchell's departure by running a story identifying the attorney as comptroller of a CREEP secret intelligence fund worth as much as $700,000 in undeclared tax donations. Nixon campaign finance chairman, Maurice H. Stans, disbursed the money from his office safe. Somebody got rid of the one-page, hand written ledger of where the cash went, but investigators were patient and pieced together the money trail during the next two years. Mitchell, of course, denied being comptroller of anything, calling the allegation "the most sickening thing I've ever heard."

The *Post*'s next story sickened even more people. The article described one-time Treasury Department attorney, Donald H. Segretti, as a CREEP employee, hired to spy, disrupt Democratic political rallies, and make false accusations to discredit Democratic candidates. When questioned, Segretti revealed details of the "dirty tricks" initiative. He told investigators that the White House sanctioned what he was doing and named the President's appointment secretary, Dwight L. Chapin, as one of his contacts.

The highly publicized Watergate burglary trial concluded in January 1973, six months after the break-in. Of the seven men indicted, five pleaded guilty to charges of breaking and entering, con-

themselves very quickly."

spiracy, and wiretapping. McCord and Liddy held out, choosing to take their chances at trial. They were subsequently convicted of the same charges.

Trial Judge John C. Sirica spoke throughout the proceedings about his doubts concerning the truthfulness of the testimonies of the Watergate defendants. He opined that the break-in at the Watergate was part of a much larger conspiracy in political espionage. When the guilty verdict came in, Sirica sentenced each of the defendants to twenty to forty years, the maximum allowed by federal law. Some thought the stiff sentence was a blatant attempt to get the seven to spill their guts for favorable consideration at final sentencing.

James McCord was first to bite. In a letter that Sirica later released publicly, McCord confessed that he and the other defendants were under tremendous pressure to plead guilty and keep their mouths shut. McCord said that people "high up" were involved in the Watergate burglary. He fingered John Dean and John Mitchell as the persons who ordered him to commit perjury. He also said he and his cohorts were offered money in exchange for their silence. And so, James McCord became the first in a long line of witnesses who offered to testify in hopes of staying out of jail.

The five guilty pleas and two convictions resulting from the botched burglary at the Watergate Hotel and Office Complex became the atom about to explode into a mushroom cloud toxic enough to sweep out the White House and selected portions of Capitol Hill. Judge John Sirica's proceedings, and growing Democratic outrage, combined to compel the U.S. Senate to unanimously decide to form the Select Committee on Presidential Campaign Activities. The Justice Department joined in by seating a special federal grand jury.

The Nixon administration found itself in disarray. A bitter battle had developed in Sirica's courtroom when White House aide Alexander Butterfield, when testifying before Congress, inadvertently disclosed the existence of secret presidential tape recordings of conversations between those who may have been involved in the Watergate fiasco. President Nixon approached John Dean, asking him to fall on the sword by signing a statement admitting he was the principal architect of the cover-up. Dean refused to take the rap, openly threatening to testify if he was made scapegoat. On April 30, 1973, the President held a press conference announcing the resignations of H.R. Haldeman, John Ehrlichman, and Attorney General Richard Kleindienst (who, seemingly, was only a victim of "guilt by association"). Nixon insisted the resignations in no way implied the men's guilt in any way, only that the distractions of the investigation prevented them from doing their jobs effectively. The same day, the President released a brief statement announcing John Dean's termination.

Republicans everywhere drew a cautious breath of relief. Still believing Nixon's repeated denial of knowledge of the Watergate cover-up, they hoped the dismissals would satisfy investigators enough to stop the digging and put the scandal to rest. But the firings had the opposite effect. Because of the departures, new Attorney General Elliott Richardson found himself under increased pressure to appoint a special prosecutor. On May 25, Archibald Cox, Richardson's former law professor at Harvard, received the appointment, and with it, the Justice Department files on the Watergate investigation.

John Dean wanted to stay out of jail, and he wanted to keep his law license in the process, so he volunteered to testify before the committee—if he was granted immunity from prosecution. Dean claimed he was only acting on his superior's orders while trying to be a loyal employee. Dean told Cox's investigators Nixon had warned him "in the strongest terms" to protect the secrets of covert activities within the Nixon administration. He also testified that he spoke with President Nixon about the cover-up on at least thirty-five different occasions, usually in the Oval Office.

Special Prosecutor Cox subpoenaed the tapes made of business in Nixon's office. That the tapes even existed shocked most everyone. Apparently, Nixon had installed the voice tap equipment throughout the White House and at Camp David for posterity some time in 1971. Only a few of his closest advisors knew about them. Ironically, the tapes became the most damning evidence in proving Nixon's involvement in Watergate.

The tapes were obviously key to the investigation, so Sirica wasted no time in issuing an order for their immediate release to the Senate committee and the grand jury. Claiming executive privilege, Nixon ignored the order. Sirica appealed, and the U.S. Court of Appeals affirmed the order, directing Nixon to turn over the tapes. Again, Nixon refused, but this time he offered a compromise: he would allow Democratic Senator Stennis to listen to the tapes and then approve an edited version for investigators. Cox all but laughed at the "deal" and demanded the unedited tapes be immediately released. When Nixon refused to honor another subpoena on July 26, 1973, a showdown developed between executive and judicial branches of the federal government.

Meanwhile, back at the White House, Nixon tried to calm an ever-growing outraged American public. He appeared on television staunchly defending his right to refuse their release. His office released over one thousand pages of edited transcripts, which, even with redactions, gave the public a rather disturbing glimpse into Dick Nixon's Oval Office. The transcripts revealed an embattled chief executive living in a gangland-style atmosphere of tough language and loyal henchmen who plotted reprisals against perceived enemies. Profanities were so prevalent throughout the text, readers grew bored with the number of times they came across "expletive deleted."

Demand for full disclosure increased. Nixon released the tapes in a piecemeal fashion. By November of 1973, investigators revealed that one of the tapes contained eighteen minutes of unexplained silence. Rose Mary Woods, Nixon's long-time personal secretary, testified before the Congressional Committee that she had "accidentally" deleted the eighteen minutes of conversation while transcribing the content. The next day she raised a few eyebrows by amending her story, saying she was not responsible for more than five minutes of the missing tape. The committee sent the tapes to a panel of electronic voice recording experts who determined the missing content was caused by at least five separate erasures, indicating purposeful tampering. No one would say who was responsible.

Dick nervously pled his case. "I had no prior knowledge of the Watergate break-in," he told a suspicious nationwide television audience on August 15, 1973. I neither took part in nor knew about any of the subsequent cover-up activities. I neither authorized nor encouraged subordinates to engage in illegal or improper campaign tactics. That was, and is, the simple truth."

By now nobody was buying the President's story, especially

without the missing eighteen minutes. He had to be aware the missing tape would prove or disprove his innocence, but Nixon held on to the executive privilege excuse and refused to comply with the court order or the special prosecutor. But he wasn't the only one stonewalling investigators. The ever-growing list of White House witnesses also tried to avoid testifying before Sam Ervin's committee by invoking "executive privilege." Ervin wasn't having any of it, however, and announced anybody trying to dodge a subpoena based on the excuse would be smacked with a charge of contempt of Congress.

Finally desperate, Nixon ordered Cox to stop pursuing the tapes. When Cox refused, Nixon initiated what later became known as the "Saturday night massacre," another apparently ill-thought-out order, this time for Attorney General Richardson to fire Cox for insubordination. Wisely, Richardson responded with his immediate resignation rather than fire his old professor. Undaunted, "Tricky Dickie," as he was becoming known, jumped down a rung and ordered Deputy Attorney General William D. Ruckelshaus to give Cox his walking papers. Ruckelshaus also refused, and he was summarily fired. Nixon continued down the ladder until he found Solicitor General Robert Bork, who finally gave Attorney Cox the boot.

The Saturday night massacre all but convicted Tricky Dickie in the court of public opinion. Editorial pages across the country flared with allegations of presidential corruption and abuses of executive power. Critics called for Nixon's resignation, and there were murmurs of impeachment all around Congress. Sensing impending doom, the president's supporters, even the strongest, began to distance themselves from him. On March 17, 1974, the federal grand jury assigned to Watergate indicted seven former Nixon administration officials on charges of conspiracy to obstruct justice: H.R. Haldeman, John Ehrlichman, John Mitchell, Charles W. Colson, Gordon Strachan, Robert C. Mardian, and Kenneth W. Parkinson. John Dean, Jeb Magruder, and several lesser players had already pleaded guilty. The grand jury report also named Richard M. Nixon as an "unindicted co-conspirator."

On June 3, Colson, a White House special counsel, pleaded guilty to charges related to the Ellsberg case. Colson claimed he was only following President Nixon's order. Nixon's last-ditch effort to protest the eighteen minutes of tape ended on July 24, when the Supreme Court ruled eight to none that the President had to surrender any of the tapes that may contain evidence in the trials of his former

The Burglar Recidivist

RICHARD NIXON'S FIRST FORAY INTO BREAKING and entering occurred when he was a young man attending the Duke University Law School. Then known as "Gloomy Gus" to his friends, he participated in his first known office burglary.

Gloomy Gus and two pals were at the top of their class. Exams were over, and the trio could hardly wait to see their final grades. So they didn't wait. The three future lawyers conspired to break into the dean's office and take a peek at their grades.

They met outside the dean's office door. Two of the guys lifted the third up on their shoulders, so he could climb through the open transom and unlock the door from inside. Once inside, they rummaged around and found the filing cabinet keys, where they could find the still-secret grades and final class rankings. They looked, learned which of them ranked first, and then slithered away as quietly as they came.

Gloomy Gus pulled off his first caper, perhaps emboldening him for later break-ins. Unfortunately for him, he wasn't as successful at the Watergate Office Complex, and "Gloomy Gus" became "Tricky Dick." ✪

subordinates. Cornered, Nixon appointed Texas attorney Leon Ja-worski the new special prosecutor and agreed to release the tapes to Judge Sirica and Congress.

The House Judiciary Committee opened formal debate on Nixon's impeachment on July 24. It only took three days for the committee to approve Article I of an impeachment resolution, accusing Nixon of obstruction of justice, by a vote of twenty-seven to eleven. Article II, charges of systematic abuse of power and violations of citizen's civil rights regarding the 1969-1971 wiretapping program, was approved by a vote of twenty-eight to ten on July 29. Article III, charging Nixon with contempt of Congress, was adopted the next day by a vote of twenty-one to seventeen. Two other articles were rejected.

Back against a hard wall, Nixon turned over the remaining tapes from the Oval Office on August 5. They became known as the "smoking gun" because they provided final, irrefutable proof linking Nixon to the crimes. The tapes spotlighted Tricky Dickie himself as ordering a full-scale cover-up of the Watergate break-in. They also proved he was well aware of White House involvement in CREEP.

Upon hearing the "smoking gun" recordings, the eleven Republicans on the Judiciary Committee changed their votes on the articles of impeachment from no to yes. The truth was in the tapes. Dick Nixon faced certain impeachment by the House and conviction in the Senate.

Facing the inevitable reality that he'd be the first U.S. President in history to be thrown out of the Oval Office, on August 8, 1974, Richard M. Nixon decided to cash in what chips he still had left and resign. He spoke from the Oval Office by television, telling America:

> By taking this action, I hope I will have hastened the start
> of the process of healing which is so desperately needed

in America . . . . I hereby resign the office of President of the United States."

Unlike numerous members of his administration, some of whom were close personal friends, Richard Nixon was never convicted of any crime or served one day of prison time. One month later, Gerald Ford, who was serving the remainder Nixon's term as president, granted the former-president "full, free, and absolute pardon" for crimes he committed while in office.

Many in the country were outraged, feeling that Nixon had escaped justice, and any hope of Ford winning the White House in 1976 was dashed. Trickie Dick seemed to have won in the end—or at least was not punished. He also never showed the sort of remorse the country wanted to see.

President Richard M. Nixon

Tricky Dick's Quotable Quips

MOST PEOPLE THINK RICHARD NIXON SCREWED HIMSELF BY secretly taping official conversations in the Oval Office and elsewhere because the recordings ultimately proved, after previous denials, that he knew all about the Watergate cover-up. Those tapes also revealed a candid and up-too-close view that further damaged the Nixon legacy—revealing him to be not only corrupt but a racist, a sexist and various other *ists*. Here are a few other quotable quips from President Dick's Big Book of White House Wit & Wisdom.

On Women: "I don't think women should be in any government job whatever. I mean, I really don't. The reason why I do is mainly because they are erratic and emotional."

On Jews: "The Jews are irreligious, atheistic, immoral bunch of bastards."

On African-Americans: "I have the greatest affection for them, but I know they're not going to make it for five hundred years. They aren't. You know it, too."

On Mexican-Americans: "The Mexicans are a different cup of tea. They have a heritage. At the present time they steal, they're dishonest, but they do have some concept of family life."

On Homosexuals: "You know what happened to the Romans? The last six Roman emperors were fags. Neither in a public way. You know what happened to the popes? They were laying the nuns; that's been going on for years, centuries. But the Catholic Church went to hell three or four centuries ago. It was homosexual, and it had to be cleaned out. That's what's happened to Britain. It happened earlier to France.

Let's look at the strong societies. The Russians. Goddamn, they root 'em out. They don't let 'em around at all. I don't know what they do with them. Look at this country. You think the Russians allow dope? Homosexuality, dope, immorality are the enemies of strong societies. That's why the Communists and left-wingers are clinging to one another. They're trying to destroy us.

On Invoking Executive Privilege: "I don't give a shit what happens. I want you all to stonewall it, let them plead the Fifth Amendment, cover-up, or anything else, if it'll save it—save the plan. That's the whole point."

On Legalizing Marijuana: "You know, it's a funny thing, every one of the bastards that are out for legalizing marijuana are Jewish. What the Christ is the matter with the Jews, Bob? What is the matter with them? I suppose it is because most of them are psychiatrists."

On Jews and Communism: "Many Jews in the Communist conspiracy. . . . Chambers and Hiss were the only non-Jews. . . . Many thought that Hiss was. He could have been a half. . . . Every other one was a Jew — and it raised hell for us. But in this case, I hope to God he's not a Jew."

On African-Americans & Communism: "So few of those who engage in espionage—are Negroes. . . . In fact, very few of them become Communists. If they do, they like, they get into Angela Davis—they're more the capitalist type. And they throw bombs and this and that. But the Negroes—have you ever noticed? Any Negro spies?"

On Women in the Workplace: "I'm not for women, frankly, in any job. I don't want any of them around. Thank God we don't have any in the Cabinet."

On Jews as Justices on the Supreme Court: "As long as I'm sitting in the chair, there's not going to be any Jew appointed to that court. [No Jew] can be right on the criminal-law issue."

On Securing Surrender of the North Vietnamese: "I call it the Madman Theory, Bob. I want the North Vietnamese to believe I've reached the point where I might do anything to stop the war. We'll just slip the word to them that, for God's sake, you know Nixon is obsessed about Communism. We can't restrain him when he's angry—and he has his hand on the nuclear button—and Ho Chi Minh himself will be in Paris in two days begging for peace."

On Nuclear War (during a conversation with Henry Kissinger):

Nixon: I still think we ought to take the North Vietnamese dikes out now. Will that drown people?

Kissinger: About two hundred thousand people.

Nixon: No, no, no, I'd rather use the nuclear bomb. Have you got that, Henry?

Kissinger: That, I think, would just be too much.

Nixon: The nuclear bomb, does that bother you? . . . I just want you to think big, Henry, for Christ sakes. . . . The only place where you and I disagree . . . is with regard to the bombing. You're so goddamned concerned about civilians and I don't give a damn. I don't care.

Kissinger: I'm concerned about the civilians because I don't want the world to be mobilized against you as a butcher.

On Welfare Reform: "We're going to [put] more of these little Negro bastards on the welfare rolls at $2,400 a family—let people like Pat Moynihan and [special consultant] Leonard Garment and others believe in all that crap. But I don't believe in it. Work, work—throw 'em off the rolls. That's the key."

On Homosexuality on Television: "I don't mind the homosexuality. I understand it. Nevertheless, goddamn, I don't think you glorify it on public television, homosexuality, even more than you glorify whores. We all know we have weaknesses. But, goddammit, what do you think that does to kids? You know what happened to the Greeks! Homosexuality destroyed them. Sure, Aristotle was a homo. We all know that. So was Socrates."

On San Francisco: "It is the most faggy goddamned thing you could ever imagine, with that San Francisco crowd. I can't shake hands with anybody from San Francisco."

On Fashion Designers: "One of the reasons fashions have made women look so terrible is because the goddamned designers hate women. Designers taking it out on the women."

On the State Department's Posture on Equal Opportunity: "Screw State! State's always on the side of the blacks. The hell with them!"

On Abortion: "There are times when an abortion is necessary. I know that. When you have a black and a white. Or a rape."

And now, a few quotes about Nixon.

"Mr. Nixon lacks the moral sensitivity which the occupant of the White House should possess . . . he is impetuous, quick to act, rash, and on occasion his conduct is irresponsible."

"Richard Nixon is a no good, lying bastard. He can lie out of both sides of his mouth at the same time, and if he ever caught himself telling the truth, he'd lie just to keep his hand in."

"Nixon is a shifty-eyed goddamn liar. He's one of the few in the history of this country to run for high office talking out of both sides of his mouth at the same time and lying out of both sides."

"He is a dangerous man. Never has there been one like him so close to the presidency."

"A mean, nasty fellow."

"I don't like Nixon and I never will."

—*Harry S. Truman on Richard Nixon*

"In his memoirs Nixon declared that to achieve his ends the 'institutions' of government had to be 'reformed, replaced or circumvented. In my second term I was prepared to adopt whichever of these three methods — or whichever combination of them — was necessary'." —*Sidney Blumenthal*

"Richard Nixon was the most dishonest person I ever met in my entire life."—*Barry Goldwater*

"Boys, I may not know much, but I know chicken shit from chicken salad."—*Lyndon B. Johnson, to reporters after hearing a Nixon speech.*

"Do you realize the responsibility I carry? I'm the only person standing between Richard Nixon and the White House."—*John F. Kennedy during the 1960 presidential campaign.*

"Nixon's comments about Jews were sort of—there was a huge disparity between the comments he made about Jews and the large number of Jews he had in his administration. And it is hard to believe in one sense. I don't really think Nixon was anti-Semitic. He had sort of standard phrases."—*Henry Kissinger*

"He has a technique that I am disconcerted with, because he appears so forthright, all the time, as soon as he get entangled, he tries to get sentimental. He tries to distance himself from a response by turning sentimental, and that I find very difficult."—*Former Swedish Prime Minister Olof Palme*

"He was captured by TV, that was how he tried to connect with the American people. One of the few times I've met him was at Pompidou's funeral, right before the end. There was a TV in the church. He [Nixon] had a half-centimeter-thick layer of pancake, or make-up, because there could be TV-cameras around. It looked completely macabre, you could barely see the face. I was conversing with him, and it was like speaking to a mask."—*Former Swedish Prime Minister Olof Palme*

"The President wants me to argue that he is as powerful a monarch as Louis XIV, only four years at a time, and is not subject to the processes of any court in the land except the court of impeachment." —*James D. St. Clair, Richard Nixon's counsel, arguing before the Supreme Court*

"If the right people had been in charge of Nixon's funeral, his casket would have been launched into one of those open-sewage canals that empty into the ocean just south of Los Angeles. He was a swine of a man and a jabbering dupe of a president. Nixon was so crooked that he needed servants to help him screw his pants on every morning. His body should have been burned in a trash bin."—*Hunter S. Thompson.*

"The kind of guy that could shake your hand and stab you in the back at the same time."—*Hunter S. Thompson.*

"I've been called worse things by better people."—*Canadian Prime Minister Pierre Trudeau on hearing that he had been called "that asshole" by Nixon.* ✪

Fun with Dick and Jane

JANE FONDA WAS DEEPLY EMBROILED IN HER ANTI-war efforts in 1970 when she returned from a rally in Ontario, Canada, on November 2 by way of Cleveland's Hopkins International Airport. Upon her arrival in the States, customs officials discovered one hundred and five vials of pills in Fonda's luggage. Assuming the activist actress was smuggling drugs into the country, they promptly took her into custody at an airport security office. There she allegedly assaulted a security officer while being detained. She was eventually booked into the Cuyahoga County Jail on charges of drug smuggling and assault. The arrest made front-page headlines around the country, which was deeply divided about the Vietnam War in general and Fonda's activities in particular.

When both charges were dropped, the story, if it was reported at all, seldom showed up before page six of the news. But that wasn't the end of the story, according to Jane Fonda. In her 2005 autobiography *My Life So Far*, Fonda claims she was the target of a government operation organized to disrupt anti-war protesters activities through a secret operation known as COINTELPRO.

Ms. Fonda describes COINTELPRO as a counter-intelligence program dreamed up by the Nixon administration and Federal Bureau of Investigation director J. Edgar Hoover to "discredit members of the antiwar and militant black movements." She says COINTELPRO worked by ". . . infiltration, sabotage, intimidation, murder (directly assassinating or hiring rival groups to assassinate leaders), by framing activists for crimes the FBI committed, and through fake black propaganda—feeding journalists information through phony letters and inflammatory leaflets that slandered and discredited the targeted person."

Other than some negative publicity and fearful inconvenience on Jane Fonda's part, nothing came of the incident at the Cleveland airport. As for COINTELPRO's alleged efforts against the Hollywood star, Fonda concludes, "After extensive investigation of COINTELPRO, Senator Frank Church's Select Committee on Government Intelligence Activities pronounced it 'a sophisticated vigilante program aimed squarely at preventing the exercise of First Amendment rights of freedom and association.' Seems the government felt it necessary to destroy democracy in order to save it. And look where it got us—Watergate and the first Presidential resignation in U.S. history." ✪

9

The Only Good Commie . . .

THE BIGGEST SCANDAL OF RONALD Reagan's era in the White House occurred in 1984 with the Iran–Contra affair, a cash-for-weapons, three-way scheme to fund anti-communism efforts in Central America. When Reagan took office in 1981 he already saw a threat in Nicaragua, when the pro-communist Sandinista revolutionaries overthrew Anastasia Somoza Garcia in 1978. The new president immediately sought ways to support the Sandinistas' main opponents, known as Contras, a poorly organized armed group of resisters. By 1981, President Reagan made the Contras' success his

President Ronald Reagan

highest priority in Western Hemisphere foreign policy. He signed authorization for the CIA to conduct "political and paramilitary operations" against the Sandinistas. Reagan even fibbed to Congress, saying the funds he requested were to be used to keep arms out of Central America.

The ever-increasing amount of cash spent on arms "interdiction" aroused suspicions in Congress by December of 1982. The legislature promptly enacted the first two versions of the Boland Act. Named for the Massachusetts representative and chairman of the House Select Committee on Intelligence, Edward Boland, the measure specifically prohibited the CIA and the Defense Department from spending American dollars to overthrow the Sandinistas or to promote conflict between Nicaragua and its neighbor Honduras, a haven for Contra bases.

Despite the Boland Act, CIA-backed operatives participated in mining Nicaragua's harbors. When the Senate Intelligence Committee caught wind of the CIA's actions, they called CIA Director William Casey, a former Reagan campaign chairman and veteran World World II spy, to explain the CIA's activities in Central America. As a result, Casey agreed to consult the committee before any initiation of covert activities. The agreement, known as the Casey accord, had no guarantees other than Casey's word.

Unsatisfied, Congress amended the Boland Act to stem the flow of arms to Nicaragua. Specifically, the amendment forbade any U.S. intelligence agency from furnishing lethal aid to the Contras. The Reagan administration refused to give up on the Contra cause and decided to enlist the National Security Council (NSC), an agency answerable only to the President himself (and with no obligations to the legislature), to take over the Contra cause. The NSC chose Marine Colonel Oliver North, a decorated veteran of Vietnam and the Grenada campaigns, to oversee Contra-related operations. They called the project "Enterprise."

Under Casey's guidance, Colonel North devised a number of complex operations designed to raise money for the Contras. Enterprise sold weapons to Iran, negotiated for the release of Americans held in the Middle East, and provided military strategies for pro-U.S. forces in Nicaragua. North enlisted retired Air Force General Richard Secord and native Iranian banker Albert Hakim to assist in the newly formed "Project Democracy." Secord was well-versed and maintained contacts in the intelligence community while Hakim could establish a web of overseas bank accounts and front companies through which money could be laundered. Casey, North, Secord, and Hakim formed the core of Operation Democracy activities.

The effort raised nearly $48 million in two years, a quarter of which was available for weapons for the Contras after expenses. The Contra rebels grew into a well-armed, if largely unorganized, band of fighters. North arranged for a Contra airstrip to be built in neighboring Costa Rica, establishing a southern front for the rebel cause. Project Democracy continued to grow. North managed to establish an intelligence network inside Nicaragua by hiring a company known as the Institute for Democracy, Education, and Assistance and then arranging for the cover group to receive a government contract through the State Department's Nicaraguan Humanitarian Assistance Office. The contract, of course, was nothing more than a cover for the intelligence operation. The project was operational when North hired former Air Force pilot Richard Gadd to airlift supplies into the country.

But as the operation grew, so did its profile in the public eye— through rumors and mentions in the press. Members of Congress queried National Security Advisor Robert McFarlane about the rumors, but he repeatedly lied. The enterprise continued to grow.

Other than the Contras, President Reagan's foreign policy concerns included a number of Americans who were held hostage in Lebanon and other parts of the Middle East. Their captors were radical Shiite Muslims with ties to Iran. Relations between the U.S. and Iran were at an all-time low. Iran saw the United States as "the great Satan," and President Reagan referred to Iran as part of "a new, international version of Murder Incorporated." The Enterprise became involved in the hostage situation by suggesting they broker a deal with the Iranians. McFarlane contacted Israeli intelligence officer David Kimche to discuss an arms-for-hostages deal.

Kimche contacted Iranian Manucher Ghobanifar as a middleman for the swap. Ghobanifar, known to the CIA as untrustworthy and self-serving, used his connection to Casey's friend Roy Furmark to get in on the plot. In mid-September of 1985, hostage Reverend Benjamin Weir was released. The part of the puzzle Americans didn't know was that Weir's freedom came at a price: five hundred TOW anti-tank missiles. Seeing success, the Enterprise tried for more hostages by sending HAWK anti-aircraft missiles from Israel to Iran. But claiming the cargo was defective, the Iranians reneged and no hostages were released.

Rumors of the arms-for-hostages scheme reached both Secretary of State George Shultz and Secretary of Defense Caspar Weinberger, who both advised the President to put an immediate halt to similar operations. Reagan ignored the advice. The Enterprise rolled on.

Because the Iranians rejected the previous deal, the Enterprise decided to cut out Israel as the middleman. Negotiations would now be handled directly between North and the Iranians. As the transactions progressed, North noticed the Enterprise was now turning a profit. He decided it was a good idea to use the funds to the benefit of the Contra cause. The link between two nations, half a world apart, formed. Weapons sales for the Contras generated more than $3.8 million for the cause.

Admiral John Poindexter took over the NSC when McFarlane left in late 1985. In May 1986, McFarlane traveled to Tehran to negotiate for the release of more hostages. He left empty handed several days later. Iran had upped the ante by demanding the release of Shiite Muslims jailed in Kuwait. Surprisingly, despite the Iranians refusal to play ball, weapons shipments continued.

The Enterprise began to fall apart on October 5, 1986, when a C-123 cargo plane loaded with weapons and supplies for the Contras was shot down over Nicaragua. Three crewmembers died in the crash. The lone survivor, Eugene Hasenfus, became a Sandinista prisoner. Documents in the downed plane revealed that it was owned by Southern Air Transport, a Miami-based CIA front company. The incident immediately triggered investigations by the FBI, the U.S. Customs Service, Congress, and the media. At the same time, the Lebanese magazine *Al Shiraa* ran a story about Robert McFarlane's visit to Iran. The speaker of the Iranian parliament confirmed the article.

President Reagan hit the airwaves in an attempt to minimize the situation. Too late! Attorney General Edwin Meese compounded the fiasco by trying to create a plausible explanation out of lies and half-truths. Documents that Meese couldn't use were ordered destroyed. The NSC held all-night shredding parties. Oliver North's secretary, Fawn Hall, even smuggled some papers out of the Old Executive Building in her bra and panties.

Despite the shredding mania, Justice Department investigators found a memo in NSC files directing that funds from the sale of arms would be diverted to the Contras. Attorney General Meese met with the key players to discuss fallout and damage control. By November 25, the President announced the formation of a "special review committee" to be headed by former Republican Texas Senator John Tower. The panel also included former Secretary of State Edwin Muskie and National Security Advisor Brent Scowcroft. Three months of investigations resulted in the three-hundred-page Tower Commission report that criticized President Reagan's judgment in leadership. But the report couldn't stop a Congressional investigation or the appointment of an independent counsel, Lawrence Walsh.

The Congressional investigations were highly publicized and televised across the nation. Detailed descriptions of what occurred inside the NSC were broadcast coast to coast. In an effort to get to the heart of the matter—and gather information Democrats wanted to exploit politically—Congress granted Poindexter and North limited immunity from prosecution. Poindexter protected the President by denying he had told anyone at the White House about Enterprise's activities. He told the committee "he couldn't remember" specific details of the operation one hundred and seventy-five times during questioning. For his part, McFarlane admitted lying to Congress in the past. Casey never testified because he died on May 6, 1987, while recuperating from brain surgery.

Oliver North's televised testimony provided the highlight of the hearings. Dressed in his Marine officer's uniform, North recounted details of his job, maintaining he was authorized by the highest-ranking administrators to carry them out. It's still unclear today whether or not President Reagan ever realized that the arms-for-hostages scheme really meant funds for the Contras.

The independent counsel's investigation took five-and-a-half years and cost $32 million. It resulted in North's being found guilty of obstructing Congress, destroying government documents, and accepting an illegal gratuity—a security fence at his home he felt he needed to protect his family from threats made by a little-known Islamic militant named Osama Bin Laden. An appeals court later reversed North's convictions, ruling that Lawrence Walsh had developed his case using North's immunized testimony. Poindexter was the only other principal player convicted—for lying to Congress. Some of the lesser figures also drew convictions on various charges from lying to Congress to unlawfully withholding information.

As the investigation rolled on, the public began to lose interest—the whole affair seemed so complicated and convoluted that most people moved on to other news. The whole ordeal ended in 1992 when President George H. W. Bush granted full and complete pardons to all those involved in "Iran–Contra."

10

Bill Soils a Blue Dress

THE WHITEWATER SCANDAL, INVOLVING
Bill and Hillary Clinton's real estate investments in
the 1970s and 1980s, introduced independent
counsel Kenneth Starr to the wonderful world of
presidential woes for William Jefferson Clinton.
Along the way while looking into Whitewater,
Starr learned that the President was involved in
a web of lies regarding a sexual harassment
lawsuit pressed against him by Paula Jones.
The President allegedly lied during a deposition
about the sexual affair he had with White House
intern Monica Lewinsky and his inducement of
Monica to lie in an affidavit by denying the

affair. Starr learned about the President's tryst with Lewinsky when Linda Tripp, a former White House staffer, turned over tape recordings she had made of conversations with Monica. The tapes, which Lewinsky didn't know about, revealed lurid details of Monica and Bill's boinking sessions, including the existence of a semen-stained dress. Bill maintained nothing happened. He firmly scolded members of the media when he asserted, "I did not have sexual relations with that woman, Miss Lewinsky!"

On September 9, 1998, Starr released his report to the House of Representatives, indicating: "There is substantial and credible information that President Clinton committed acts that may constitute grounds for an impeachment." Two days later, members of the House voted three hundred and sixty-three to sixty-three to make the report public, even though most representatives didn't bother to read it. Hours later, the report was available in its entirety over the Internet. Even though parts of the report read like a cheap porn novel, they made it into print for the public's consideration. (Example: "There, according to Ms. Lewinsky, they kissed. She was wearing a long dress that buttoned from the neck to the ankles. 'And he unbuttoned my dress and he unhooked my bra, and sort of took the dress off my shoulders and . . . moved the bra . . . . [H]e was looking at me and touching me and telling me how beautiful I was.' He touched her breasts with his hands and his mouth, and touched her genitals, first through underwear and then directly. She performed oral sex on him.")

The House voted two hundred and fifty-nine to one hundred and seventy-six to begin an impeachment inquiry. House Judiciary Committee Chairman Henry Hyde of Illinois announced on October 14 that the inquiry would focus on perjury witness tampering and obstruction of justice.

On November 13, Clinton reached a settlement with Paula Jones. Six days later, Starr answered questions about his referral to the House committee. In written answers to committee questions,

Clinton denied any lies. The Starr report elaborates on President Clinton's rationale:

> Testifying before the grand jury on August 17, 1998, seven months after his Jones deposition, the President acknowledged "inappropriate intimate contact" with Ms. Lewinsky but maintained that his January deposition testimony was accurate. In his account, "what began as a friendship [with Ms. Lewinsky] came to include this conduct." He said he remembered "meeting her, or having my first real conversation with her during the government shutdown in November of '95." According to the President, the inappropriate contact occurred later

Starr learned the president was involved in a web of lies

> (after Ms. Lewinsky's internship had ended), "in early 1996 and once in early 1997."
>
> The President refused to answer questions about the precise nature of his intimate contacts with Ms. Lewinsky, but he did explain his earlier denials. As to his denial in the Jones deposition that he and Ms. Lewinsky had had a "sexual relationship," the President maintained that there can be no sexual relationship without sexual intercourse, regardless of what other sexual activities may transpire. He stated that "most ordinary Americans' would embrace this distinction.
>
> The President also maintained that none of his sexual contacts with Ms. Lewinsky constituted "sexual relations" within a specific definition used in the Jones deposition. Under that definition: [A] person engages in

"sexual relations" when the person knowingly engages in or causes—(1) contact with the genitalia, anus, groin, breast, inner thigh, or buttocks of any person with an intent to arouse or gratify the sexual desire of any person. . . . "Contact" means intentional touching, either directly, or through clothing.

According to what the President testified was his understanding, this definition "covers contact by the person being deposed with the enumerated areas, if the contact is done with an intent to arouse or gratify," but it does not cover oral sex performed on the person being deposed. He testified:

[I]f the deponent is the person who has oral sex performed on him, then the contact is with—not with anything on that list, but with the lips of another person. It seems to be self-evident that that's what it is. . . . Let me remind you, sir, I read this carefully.

In the President's view, "any person, reasonable person" would recognize that oral sex performed on the deponent falls outside the definition.

If Ms. Lewinsky performed oral sex on the President, then—under this interpretation—she engaged in sexual relations but he did not. The President refused to answer whether Ms. Lewinsky in fact had performed oral sex on him. He did testify that direct contact with Ms. Lewinsky's breasts or genitalia would fall within the definition, and he denied having any such contact.

Largely along party lines, the Judiciary Committee approved four articles of impeachment, two alleging lies in the Jones case and two involving obstructing justice and abuse of power in the Lewinsky case, to be sent to the House floor. Only two articles of impeachment made it to a Senate trial.

White House Wisdom

PRESIDENTS SOMETIMES EXHIBIT A ZEN-LIKE wisdom in their comments to the American people. Other times they just sound sort of stupid. Here is a short list of enigmatic statements that left audiences scratching their heads:

For those who like this sort of thing, this is the sort of thing they like. – *Abraham Lincoln*

When large numbers of men are unable to find work, unemployment results. – *Calvin Coolidge*

Always be sincere, even if you don't mean it. —*Harry Truman*

Things are more like they are now than they ever have been. —*Gerald Ford*

Abortion is advocated only by persons who have themselves been born. —*Ronald Reagan*

If we don't succeed, we run the risk of failure. —*Bill Clinton*

It's very important for folks to understand that when there's more trade, there's more commerce. —*George Bush* ✪

Formal hearings began November 19. Democrats postured on President Clinton's side, maintaining the affair with Monica Lewinsky was a private matter that didn't meet the level of an impeachable offense. Nonetheless, on December 19, Bill Clinton joined Andrew Johnson as the only two presidents to ever be officially impeached.

The Senate trial began January 7, 1999, with Chief Justice William Rehnquist presiding. It lasted a little over a month. No witnesses were called. Lawyers for both sides presented their cases. After three days of closed deliberations, the Senate said they were ready to vote on February 12. As the Chief Justice called the roll, each senator rose and announced his or her vote. President Clinton was acquitted of the perjury charge by a vote of fifty-five to forty-five. The obstruction charge went fifty to fifty. Neither article came anywhere near the two-thirds majority necessary to convict.

The whole affair with Monica Lewinsky and her hummers didn't have too much negative fallout for Bill Clinton. If anything, spending $100 million to hear lurid stories of boobs, blowjobs, and how semen stained a blue cotton dress from the Gap amounted to little more than an amusing anecdote in American political folklore. President Clinton, quite tongue in cheek, even alluded to his own resilience and to the Republicans' seeming inability to exploit his peccadilloes when he told attendees at his final presidential appearance at the White House Correspondent's Dinner:

> You know, the clock is running down on the Republicans in Congress, too. I feel for them, I do. . . . They've only got seven more months to investigate me. That's a lot of pressure. So little time, so many unanswered questions. For example, over the last few months, I've lost ten pounds. Where did they go? Why haven't I produced them to the independent counsel? How did some of them wind up on [NBC's *Meet The Press* host] Tim Russert?"

11

Pants on Fire

George W. Bush

ACCORDING TO SISSELA BOK, AUTHOR OF *Lying: Moral Choice in Public and Private Life*, a lie is "an intentionally deceptive message in the form of a statement." But, as Bok also points out, it isn't that simple. Lies can be large and small, told directly or by omission, by misstating facts, or being unfaithful to oaths and vows taken. When a lie comes from a president, it takes on epic proportions. True, lying in the White House is not a recent revelation.

History has proven presidents are perfectly capable of lying to get their way or to cover up embarrassing truths. In 1941 FDR told America in a Fireside Chat that the United States should join Great Britain in its war with Nazi Germany. Supporting his case, Roosevelt spoke of the unprovoked attack on the *USS Greer* by a German U-Boat. What he didn't say was that the *Greer* was on maneuvers with the British navy on a seek-and-destroy mission, targeting the Nazi submarine.

Shortly after America ended World War II by dropping an atomic bomb on Hiroshima, President Harry Truman broadcast the message, "The world will note that the first atomic bomb was dropped on Hiroshima, a military base. That was because we wished in this first attack to avoid, in so far as possible, the killing of civilians." In

He was the Sultan of

truth, Hiroshima was no military base, but home to over 350,000 Japanese civilians.

Richard Nixon lied about Watergate, even telling the American people, "I am not a crook!" Turns out, he was, and the fib cost him his job. And, of course, Bill "Slick Willie" Clinton, earned his nickname for accepting a series of blowjobs from a willing, even eager, Monica Lewinsky and then lying about it by saying, "I did not have sexual relations with that woman, Miss Lewinsky!" Imagine that—a man lying about a sexual affair with a woman not his wife.

In fact, a close look at every president would reveal a lie or two, a few bent truths, exaggerations, and understatements. It comes with the territory.

But George W. Bush took presidential prevarication to a whole new level. He was the Sultan of Subterfuge! Count Canard! The Splendid Spinner. A liar's liar. Consider the following list (because they have to be listed) of George W. Bush's foibles, fibs, and frauds:

1. The Iraq War:

President Bush's lies about Saddam Hussein's (remember him?) Iraq has killed and wounded thousands of American soldiers and countless Iraqi men, women, and children. But this one is much more complicated. Let's make a sub-list of Bogus-Iraqi-Bushisms:

a) "The smoking gun could be a mushroom cloud." The only mushrooms Iraq could produce were the kind that grow in the substance this statement is made of.

b) "Saddam would not let the inspectors in." Bush made this claim twice. It was quite a surprise to the hundreds of United Nations inspectors already in Iraq in 2003 who were told by the U.S. to "get out or get bombed."

c) Inferred: "Iraq has weapons of mass destruction." Well, a lot

Subterfuge! A liar's liar.

of people thought Saddam was capable of achieving his wet dream of building an arsenal of WMDs. But, everybody else thought that Iraq wasn't capable of producing any sort of credible military threat to the rest of the Middle East, much less the United States. And "everybody else" included the CIA, the UN, and anyone not named Wolfowitz, Rice, Libby, Rumsfeld, Cheney, or Pearle.

d) "We know exactly where they are." That's what Bush's Defense Secretary, Donald Rumsfeld, said shortly after Bush declared "Mission Accomplished." As of this writing, President George W. Bush never got this particular memo.

e) Big words with no substance. In his 2003 State of the Union address, President Bush told the world of the horrors waiting to explode in Saddam's Iraq. Secretary of State Colin Powell read a similar laundry list at the United Nations. Powell called these charges "facts" that were unassailable. Well, George is back in the Lone Star state and General Powell, who apparently was duped and maybe a little embarrassed, didn't even stick around for W.'s second term. The "facts" turned out to be fiction.

f) "We believe that, in fact, Saddam Hussein has reconstituted nuclear weapons." Never one to mince fibs, Veep Dick Cheney said this on *Meet the Press* in 2003. Many critics of the administration felt that Cheney was the source of Bush's fibs, believing that W. wasn't capable of making up such corkers on his own.

(left) "W." enchants the crowd with words of chief executive wisdom. (above) Secretary of State Condoleeza Rice took over for Colin Powell right after W.'s re-election. Powell apparently got tired of a steady diet of crow.

g) Iraq developed "drones" that could attack the United States. Technically true, if they were launched from Isle of Palms, South Carolina. The truth is that a lot of American model airplane clubs had better capabilities than Saddam.

h) "Iraq possesses yellow cake uranium." The Italians thought the documents purporting this were fakes. For God's sake, THE ITALIANS thought the documents were fakes!

i) Our military "will be welcomed as liberators." Tell that to the more-than-three-thousand U.S. soldiers who have died after receiving far less "welcome" in Iraq.

j) Al Qaeda and Saddam Hussein had close ties. Well, both Saddam and Osama are/were Sunni Muslims, they both have/had moustaches, and they both seem/seemed to like shooting guns on TV. Other than that? Uhhhhhh. . .

k) "We have found WMDs in Iraq." It was really a portable weather tracking station/truck.

l) "They [weapons of mass destruction] could have been destroyed by Saddam. Or moved out of the country." David Kay, President Bush's handpicked inspector, said there obviously weren't any WMDs in the first place. If Bush was right and the WMDs were moved or shipped out of the country, then the whole purpose of the war—to keep Hussein from giving his WMDs to terrorists—failed! Well, George, where in the hell did they go? Did anybody tell President Obama?

The list on Iraq could continue—but why belabor the point? Let's move on.

2. Taxes, Part I

Throughout the 2000 presidential campaign and into 2001, Bush claimed his mega-tax cut for the mega-rich was really a tax cut for the working middle class. In fact, he said "the vast majority" of the money would go to "the bottom." As Al Franken pointed out at the time, "by far the vast majority" usually means more than 14.7

percent that the bottom 60 percent of Americans got. That's "fuzzy math" on a presidential level.

3. Taxes, Part II

In 2003, Bush claimed that his plans for tax cuts for the rich would create jobs. In fact, the special interest, Rockefeller tax cut was—in true Bush-spin fashion—titled the Jobs and Growth Act of 2003. Did anybody ever notice the 2.6 million jobs that "trickled down" from the tax-cut top? Anybody?

4. Taxes, Part III

Bush claimed in 2004 that if his 2001 and 2003 tax cuts for the rich were not made permanent, that the cut in itself is a tax increase! The law was written to say those taxes automatically phased out if nothing changed. Bush later said that if the law as written—the law he signed—was not changed, it amounted to an across-the-board tax increase!

5. "I fulfilled my military duty."

He said he didn't take his flight physical because his doctor was in Houston. The National Guard story never did quite seem right. The facts always remained the same, but the Bush administration's spin on the story changed with every new revelation. Despite Bush's angry denials, the issue wouldn't go away.

In his campaign autobiography, *A Charge to Keep*, W. wrote that he had completed his National Guard pilot training in 1970 and "continued flying with my unit for the next several years." But, copies of Bush's military records acquired by the *Boston Globe* said W. quit flying during his final eighteen months of a six-year hitch. They also indicated that during parts of 1972 and 1973, Bush hadn't reported for Guard duty at all. During that time, he moved to Alabama to work on a family friend's Senate campaign. During that time, he received permission to participate in "equivalent training" at an

Alabama base. Stories vary, but apparently Bush never appeared at any Alabama unit. The unit commander of the Alabama unit Bush claimed to train with told the *Globe*, that he didn't recall George W. ever showing up in Alabama. "His drill attendance should have been certified and sent to Ellington [Air Force Base in Houston], and there would have been a record. We cannot find a record to show he fulfilled the requirements in Alabama." There are only sporadic reports of Bush serving thirty-six days of service during the eighteen months at Ellington. In 1973, Bush got an early out from the Texas National Guard to attend Harvard Business School.

6. "I'm a uniter not a divider"
Bush's 2000 campaign boast—bought hook, line, and sinker by much of the media—was that only he could come to Washington and end the partisan political bickering. Within weeks of the election, however, the claim proved to be completely untrue. His heavy-handed partisanship even cost Republicans control of the U.S. Senate for a time, as Jim Jeffords bolted the party.

In 2002, Bush showed his unifying skills by saying that Democrats who disagreed with his hard-line vision for the Department of Homeland Security, a plan he had opposed for nearly a year, "didn't care about the security of the country."

Well, W. was a uniter in a way: He united the Democratic Party like never before, driving independents back in droves. Democrats now enjoy majorities in Congress, and their candidate is in the White House.

7. "I won't run a deficit."
During the 2000 campaign, Bush responded to those who said his economic plan would drive us into the Great Depression by saying that he would not operate on a deficit. He said that he was "a governor. I believe in balanced budgets." When he left office in 2009, the economy was mired in what is called the Great Recession.

There's No Lying in Baseball

PETE ROSE FOR PRESIDENT? WELL, NO, NOT REALLY. . . .
But one president did play professional baseball and later lied about it to maintain college eligibility. Fortunately, playing pro baseball doesn't disqualify a person from being president—but it could've gotten someone kicked out of college, which proved pivotal on his way to the White House.

Dwight Eisenhower is the only American president to ever play professional baseball. He played a couple of seasons for a minor league team in the Kansas State League. He apparently played the summer before becoming a plebe at West Point and another summer between his first and second years at the school. "I went into baseball deliberately to make money," he said later, "with no idea of it being a career."

Ike played center field. His name doesn't appear in league records or on any sports pages because he used the name "Wilson," knowing that any kind of professional playing experience was a violation of the amateur code, which would disqualify him from college athletics.

Of greater consequence, as a student athlete at West Point, Ike had to pledge that he'd never played professional sports. Lying violated West Point's strict honor code and would have been cause for dismissal. If Eisenhower's fib had become known, he may have never graduated to become supreme commander of the Allied forces during World War II, a job that led to his election as president.✪

8. "I'm spending less than Bill Clinton."

In an interview on *Meet the Press*, an appearance that still makes many question Bush Senior Advisor and Deputy Chief of Staff Karl Rove's sanity, Bush claimed that government spending actually dropped under his administration. Even GOP stalwarts choked on this one. The truth is that federal spending exploded under George W., just as spending exploded in Texas while he was governor. A fiscal conservative he wasn't. Consider this newspaper's quote on Bush spending:

> With his $2.23 trillion budget, his administration will complete the biggest increase in government spending since Lyndon Johnson's "Great Society."
>
> The budget deficit predicted by the House Budget Office will hit a record $306 billion. Spending on government programs increased 22% from 1999 to 2003. A *Washington Post* report said, "The era of big government, if it ever went away, has returned full-throttle under President Bush." Former House Majority Leader Dick Armey commented that under President Bush, the federal government is "out of control."
> — *Intellectual Conservative*, "Why Christians Should Not Vote for George W. Bush," February 15, 2004.

9. "No one could have imagined them hijacking airplanes."

National Security Advisor Condoleeza Rice made this claim repeatedly during the summer of 2002 in the wake of September 11. Never mind that Ramsey Yousef, one of the masterminds of the original attack on the World Trade Center, was foiled in his plot to hijack and crash twelve airplanes by U.S. and foreign intelligence agents . . . in 1995. The deceit was exposed in 2002 when details of an August 2001 President's Daily Intelligence Briefing revealed that the CIA and other sources warned the administration of just such hijackings.

10. Ken Lay

After the Enron scandal blew out of control, George W. Bush downplayed his relationship with Ken Lay saying, "he gave money to my opponent [Ann Richards]." Suddenly Lay, whom Bush had previously called "Kenny Boy," didn't ring a bell. Even though Enron and Kenny Boy were Bush's biggest contributors from 1994 to 2000, and even though Bush flew around the 1998 campaign trail in Lay's private jet, and even though Lay was a serious contender for Secretary of Commerce in a Bush White House, W. hardly knew the guy.

11. "I want to get to the bottom of the Valerie Plame leak."

Following the barrage of crap rained on Ambassador Joseph Wilson for exposing the Nigerian "yellow cake uranium" lie (see lie 1h), and the outing of his wife, Valerie Plame, as a CIA agent, Bush said it was "a very serious matter" and that he wanted to get to the bottom of it. But he never ordered his staff to do anything about it. Since very few members of the White House would have had the clearance to even know that Plame was an operative, and even fewer were permitted to talk to the media, it shouldn't have taken an expert investigator to find the culprit. But W. actually lamented that "we may never know" the identity of the snitch because "Washington is full of leakers." In the end, Lewis "Scooter" Libby, Karl Rove's lackey, took the rap, eventually convicted by a jury of perjury and obstruction of justice. His bosses escaped unscathed.

The list of Bush lies might never be complete, but only time will tell. . .

About the Author

John Boertlein has seen more than his share of sex, scandal, murder, and mayhem—and it shows. He was a police officer for nearly thirty years, achieving the rank of sergeant in the Cincinnati Police Department. He also has served in the Covington (Kentucky) and Springdale (Ohio) police departments. He holds a license to teach for the Ohio Peace Officer's Training Association and was an instructor at the Cincinnati Police Academy. He is the author of *Ohio Confidential* (Clerisy Press, 2008), in which he covers a surprising amount of sex, scandal, murder, and mayhem in the Buckeye State. He also is the author of *Howdunit: How Crimes Are Committed and Solved* (Writer's Digest Books, 2002) and *Today in History: Elvis* (Emmis Books, 2006). He lives in Cincinnati with his wife and three little yapping dogs.